Visit Tyndale's thirsty[?] Web site at areUthirsty.com

TYNDALE is a registered trademark of Tyndale House Publishers, Inc.

thirsty[?] and the thirsty[?] logo are trademarks of Tyndale House Publishers, Inc.

SHE Teen

Designed by Jacqueline L. Noe

Edited by Stephanie Voiland

Library of Congress Cataloging-in-Publication Data

St. James, Rebecca.
  SHE teen : becoming a safe, healthy, and empowered woman—God's way / Rebecca St. James and Lynda Hunter Bjorklund.
      p. cm.
  Includes bibliographical references.
  ISBN-10: 1-4143-0028-X
  ISBN-13: 978-1-4143-0028-3
  1. Teenage girls—Religious life. 2. Christian teenagers—Religious life. I. Bjorklund, Lynda Hunter. II. Title.
  BV4551.3.S75 2005
  248.8'33—dc22
                    2005005006

Printed in the United States of America

11 10 09 08 07 06 05
7 6 5 4 3 2 1

WELCOME TO THE
SHE-LIFE!

As the editor of this magazine, it's my privilege to come alongside Rebecca and talk to you about things that are important to you. It's been a couple of years since I raised my own teenage girls and far longer since I was your age myself. But many things have not changed. Satan is still after you and your friends *big* time. I've watched girls who chose to follow God's rules reap his blessings, and I've watched those who didn't follow his rules live to regret it. A lot.

I know a woman, Mona, who grew up in a Christian home, but she made a decision in her teens to turn her back on God's rules. I remember when she made that choice, and I witnessed the results. I thought you might like to hear her story, so I contacted Mona and asked her to share her experience with you. This is what she wrote:

I think I accepted Jesus at age four, and at age six I was baptized in a little country creek. My mom still recalls hearing me go to bed every night saying "Good night, Jesus." I wanted his name to be the last word out of my mouth when I went to bed and the first out of my mouth when I awoke.

At age 14, I prayed and studied my Bible before school, and I attended church regularly. I also told my friends about Jesus whenever I could.

When I was 17, I began to desire the popularity my friends had. I wondered what I was missing by not going to parties and movies I had chosen to avoid because of their content. I wanted to have a boyfriend and to be thought of as pretty. I told God, "I want to be a normal teenager." I looked at the world around me, and everyone seemed to be perfectly content with the happiness their money, popularity, and possessions brought them. Why couldn't I be like that? It doesn't mean I have to be a bad person, I thought. Just one who lives for me and no one else.

By age 19, I was getting drunk at least every weekend. But people thought of me as pretty—so much so that I had one boyfriend after another. I began to smoke and have sex. Some days I would spend hours vomiting after a night bingeing on alcohol. Everyone seemed to like me, and my life was going just the way I thought I wanted it to. But why did I feel so empty? I know—I need to get married and have children.

At 21, I found myself married to a man who physically and verbally abused me and made me feel like I was nothing. One night he stumbled into the house drunk, and we fought. Our cat and dog hid under the nearest furniture for refuge. I couldn't bring a child into a relationship like that.

I was divorced by age 26, and I moved in with my brother. We had it all, and the wild life continued. But my drinking was under control—at least I thought it was, until my DUI. Handcuffs, Miranda rights, 24 hours in jail, and the near loss of my job resulted.

By the time I was 34, I realized I had wasted half my life searching for possessions and a good job, freedom and independence— and none of them had quenched my thirst. I rededicated my life to God on his terms, not mine. I quit drinking and began this journey with him.

I am now 37 years old, and in everything I do and say, I pray God becomes greater and greater and I become less and less, for his glory. I still sometimes struggle with unconditionally giving him my will—my rule.

It means I have to put my complete faith in someone I can't see and trust that he knows what's best for me. Once as I was lying on my face before God telling him how difficult this is, I began to think of where my rules had gotten me in the past—alcohol abuse, sexual abuse, physical abuse, and a lack of respect from others and myself. My rules had given me nothing but heartache. So what was it I was afraid to give up again?

*Someone once asked me if I could go back and change something in my life, what it would be. Without hesitation, I thought of that day I told God "I want to be a normal teenager." Now I know **I am not normal. I am a child of the King.** My biggest regret is that I missed out on 17 years of growth with him. Before I was born, he knew my name. He remained faithful, even when I wasn't. It's my turn to be faithful to him.*

Now it's your turn. Your turn to make the deliberate choice to do your life God's way. Your turn to make the right decisions starting today so you won't have to try to undo some tough mistakes later on. Your turn to seek God's special blessings for you.

So what are you waiting for?

Look straight ahead, and fix your eyes on what lies before you. Mark out a straight path for your feet; stay on the safe path. Don't get sidetracked; keep your feet from following evil.

Proverbs 4:25-27

Love,
Lynda

WHO IS **SHE** ?

How can a young person stay pure?
By obeying your word.

Psalm 119:9

she:

The title every girl gets the moment she is born.

If you fully obey the LORD your God and carefully keep all his commands that I am giving you today, the LORD your God will set you high above all the nations of the world. You will experience all these blessings if you obey the LORD your God.

Deuteronomy 28:1-2

This is now bone of my bones and flesh of my flesh; SHE shall be called "woman." Genesis 2:23, NIV (emphasis added)

SHE:

The title given to those girls who seek more from God and submit their life to being transformed into his original design. The result is a Safe, Healthy, and Empowered SHE.

"When I look at models in magazines and on TV, I don't feel like I measure up."

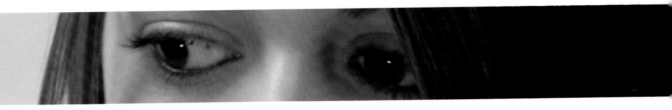

"I want to be close to God, but I don't know how."

"I feel like a lot of people in my life have let me down, and I don't know who I can trust."

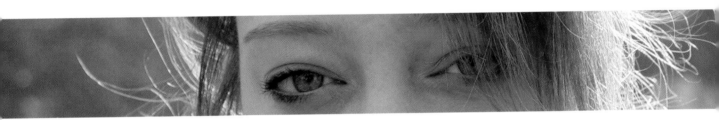

"It's sometimes hard to keep my mind and my actions pure."

"It's hard to forgive people who have hurt me."

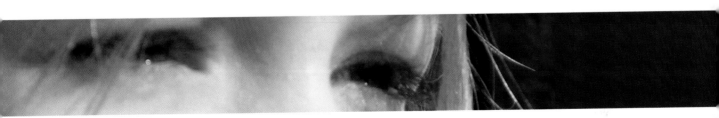

"Why am I here on this earth?"

You're not alone.

DO YOU EVER FEEL BOMBARDED BY RULES?

Rules from your parents . . .
BE HOME BY 10:00 OR YOU'RE GROUNDED.

Rules from your teachers . . .
ONE MORE TARDY AND YOU'RE STAYING AFTER SCHOOL.

Rules of the road . . .
SLOW DOWN OR YOU'RE GETTING A TICKET.

But what about your rules?

I know, you're probably thinking, *Come on, I've got enough rules already. Why would I make more for myself?* Let's stop right there and toss your old definition of rules out the window. For SHEs, our brand of rules means taking charge of your life. Making decisions for yourself. Choosing to go God's way, not the crowd's way. Believe it or not, these rules are the kind that will make you free.

As you grew up, so did the seriousness of your choices. Now you find yourself surrounded by a world offering you a menu of choices—anything you want to satisfy your appetite and any way you want to behave. The world says that you can choose your own truth, that what's right for you may not be right for me. But just so you know . . . each choice you make comes with its own consequences.

GOD'S ROAD MAP

God has provided the means for us to get to our destination. He has given us the road map—his instruction manual for life. It can help us avoid dangerous detours, dead ends, and paths that lead to places we don't want to go. Choosing the right path is based on having the right map to follow—and those choices will be guided by something solid, not on whatever feels right at the moment.

The Bible offers some rock-solid direction. Throughout the Old Testament, people had the rules God gave them for their protection. But Jesus came along and brought something more to the harsh Jewish law. He added love and mercy. Once

some rulers asked Jesus why he'd broken the rules and healed people on the Sabbath. Jesus' answer was simple: The rules were made for you, not you for the rules (Mark 2:27).

WHAT WAS HE SAYING? The mastermind who created us also created the road map to make our life work best! He loves us so much, and he wants our days on earth to go well. "Do forgive your enemies [I want you to have peace and not be eaten alive by anger]"; "Don't have sex with lots of people [I want to protect you from heartache and disease and save you for that husband I have in mind for you]." He left us the Bible, which contains our life instructions.

SHE GETS PERSONAL

Think about the following three choices you made yesterday and their possible consequences.

List everything you ate all day long. Next list possible consequences.

Describe something you said or did to a family member, a friend, or someone at school. Next list possible consequences.

Remember one thing you thought about, even if you didn't act on it. Next list possible consequences.

WHO IS SHE?

I hate those with divided loyalties, but I love your instructions. Psalm 119:113

PAGE 5

WHO IS SHE:

SHE GETS PERSONAL

One hundred years from now, only what you did for Christ will be remembered and celebrated. Everything else will be forgotten. What are you doing with your life that will be memorable for eternity?

Your life is made up of the choices you make—choice + choice + choice. Are you building the kind of life you want to live?

Your life will make a difference, either for good or bad. What kind of difference are you making?

One day Jesus will—or will not—say to you, "Well done, my good and faithful servant" (Matthew 25:21). If you really took his words to heart, how would your life change right now?

Anyone who refuses to live by these rules is not disobeying human teaching but is rejecting God, who gives his Holy Spirit to you. 1 Thessalonians 4:8

THE **CHOICES** QUIZ

I already follow God's way a whole lot better than most of my friends do. Isn't that good enough? Shouldn't God grade on a curve? Is that what you're thinking right about now? Guess what—God's standards don't quite work like our standards. Answer these questions—be honest!—and think about what exceptions you make to his guidelines.

1 At a restaurant, the waiter gives you too much change. But he was rude and didn't do a very good job. What would you do?

a) Keep the money.
b) Take the money and give it to a homeless person.
c) Politely inform the waiter of his error, then give it back.

2 You walk by a man begging on the street. You think of the dollar in your pocket, and then you think about how that man might be scamming you. What would you do?

a) Give the man the dollar.
b) Walk on by without helping the man.
c) Lecture him about how he should be finding work.

3 You're with a guy you like. He kisses you and awakens feelings you've never felt before. What would you do?

a) Keep doing what feels good.
b) Take a step back and discuss with him the lines for purity you've drawn for yourself.
c) Make excuses for your behavior and see where it goes.

Yeah, But . . .

1. Rules are no fun.
2. God's rules keep me from enjoying life.
3. No one else follows all the rules.
4. I'm sick of being told what to do.
5. Rules are too legalistic.
6. Rules mean different things to different people.
7. If I follow all of God's instructions, my friends will think I'm weird.
8. I'll have time to worry about living God's way when I get older.

You might be surprised. . . .

Those that seek me early shall find me.

Proverbs 8:17, KJV

This verse doesn't just mean to get up early and pray. It means that God reveals himself to people who dare to seek him early in their life. Before they mess up some big things. Before they do things that carry inevitable, inescapable consequences. Before they make lots of wrong choices.

Let's face it. The choices you make today will affect all your tomorrows. The choices you make today will set the pattern for your choices throughout the rest of your life.

SHE OR SHE?

No doubt you have big plans for your life. You want to be a woman who has it all—beauty, brains, and blessings. You want to be happy, successful, and loved. We're on this journey with you, and we want to let you in on a secret: the key to having good things happen to you and becoming the woman God made you to be is to follow his instructions.

This book will dig into the biggest issues we face as young women. The truth is that the Bible gives us the guidelines we need to live by. These aren't just the "don'ts" of life—they are also the "dos," and they were true long before your parents and teachers and anyone else started telling you about them. When you don't live God's way, you get what you don't want, and you don't get what you do want. When you do live by God's rules, you become the woman God created you to be.

A "she" lives her life by spineless rules or no rules at all. SHE is God-ruled. SHE follows her Creator's plan. SHE gains control of her life by giving up the controls to God. As a result, SHE proudly and confidently celebrates her womanhood.

Wait a second, you may be thinking. *I know people—good people, godly people—who have kept God's instructions but have had bad things happen to them. They get sick or the people they love let them down or they don't get what they prayed for. How can God's promises about blessing the godly and cursing the ungodly be true when these kinds of things happen?*

We understand where you're coming from. Every one of us will face hardships and disappointments, and at the time, it may seem like we aren't winning when these bad things happen. But we need to hold on to some things that are true:

Sometimes God's timing is not our timing.

Sometimes he wants us to let go of the lesser prize for the bigger one coming.

Sometimes he wants to make something better inside us that couldn't happen in comfortable circumstances.

And sometimes he's looking for that girl he can shape for the highest of callings, and that can only happen with someone he can trust to trust him—someone who will follow his ways no matter what she's facing or how long it takes.

REBECCA SAYS

I grew up in Sydney, Australia, in a wonderful Christian family. When I was eight years old, at a Girls' Brigade meeting at my church, I really felt God calling me into a living relationship with him. As well as giving my heart to him that night, I committed to living by his road map for the rest of my life. Though I haven't lived my life perfectly, I have experienced so much joy through following God's way. There is so much freedom in living the way our Creator designed us to live—as safe, healthy, and empowered young women.

The instructions of the Lord are perfect, reviving the soul. The decrees of the Lord are trustworthy, making wise the simple. The commandments of the Lord are right, bringing joy to the heart. The commands of the Lord are clear, giving insight for living. Reverence for the Lord is pure, lasting forever. The laws of the Lord are true; each one is fair. They are more desirable than gold, even the finest gold. They are sweeter than honey, even honey dripping from the comb. They are a warning to your servant, a great reward for those who obey them.
Psalm 19:7-11

Living the SHE life requires that we live with one eye on today and the other on forever. This gives us the ability to see life as God sees it and to HANG IN THERE FOR THE LONG HAUL.

QUIZ **ATTITUDE CHECK** ✓

1 PUT A CHECK MARK BESIDE ANY OF THE STATEMENTS THAT DESCRIBE YOUR ATTITUDE TOWARD RULES.

I go to church because my family expects me to.

I talk about my faith only with other Christians.

I haven't thought much about why I believe what I believe.

I mostly rely on a parent or youth leader for my spiritual growth.

My decisions (like dating boundaries, the movies I watch, and who I hang out with) are based on the standards my parent or another adult has set for me.

I don't go to church much.

I'm not comfortable talking about my faith.

I'm not really sure what I believe.

I don't have an adult in my life who gives me spiritual guidance.

My decisions (like dating boundaries, the movies I watch, and who I hang out with) are mostly based on what I'm thinking or feeling at that moment.

I used to go to church, but I feel like I've messed up too much to show my face there now.

After breaking so many of God's rules, I feel as if no one will listen to me if I share my faith.

I'm not sure if God can forgive me.

My spiritual life is kind of dead at the moment.

I've already made a lot of bad decisions (like dating boundaries, the movies I watch, and who I hang out with).

2 LOOK BACK OVER YOUR QUIZ. TOTAL UP THE CHECK MARKS FOR EACH COLUMN.

Column 1 [ ]   Column 2 [ ]   Column 3 [ ]

3 FIND OUT WHERE YOU'VE BEEN.

WHOSE RULES?

So you've heard lots of rules as you've grown up. You may have an edge on life with family and pastors and other godly people to steer you in the right direction. That's a good start, but it's not enough. There comes a time when you need to make your own list of rules—the guidelines that will define your life. It's time to graduate, girl—make those rules your own!

NO RULES?

So you haven't had godly adults to teach you godly ways. Maybe the adults you know taught you things like how to solve math problems, how to write term papers, and how to dissect frogs—but not how to live your everyday life in a healthy way. But there's good news—you still have an exciting adventure ahead of you! You have the power to make your own decisions based on your life rules. And you have the power—and the assurance—to wait patiently, knowing that when you do live by the rules, things ultimately will turn out okay.

BROKEN RULES?

So you've already messed up. Maybe you were on the right path at one time, but you've slipped along the way. There's good news! All of us have broken the rules—even your pastor and your biggest Christian hero. The Bible calls it sin (see Romans 3:12). If you ask God to forgive you, he will. But he will also help you do it better next time. You don't have to keep breaking the same rule again and again.

Who are those who fear the LORD? He will show them the path they should choose. Psalm 25:12

SHE ASKS

WHO IS SHE?

EMMA (16)

I was raised in a Christian home and have attended church and youth group regularly. But in secret, I broke many of God's rules. I lost my sexual purity. I hung out with the wrong people. And just the other day, I did something I thought I'd never do: I shoplifted with a friend. Although we didn't get caught, it scared me and made me wonder what else I would do in the future. What can I do to make up for the rules I've broken?

DID YA **KNOW . . .**

Only 44 percent of born-again adults and 9 percent of born-again 13- to 18-year-olds are certain of the existence of absolute moral truth.[1]

One out of five high school students seriously considers or attempts suicide over the course of a year.[2]

One-fourth of all abortions involve girls under 20.[3]

9 LOSER RULES OF LIFE

· I can't find anything to hold on to. I must live in fear.

· I can never get close to anyone in a healthy way.

· I've got to get all I can get, regardless of what it costs or who it hurts.

· I'll never be beautiful.

· I can't be pure and have fun.

· I've earned the right to hold on to baggage.

· I've got to go it alone.

· I can live my life out of control.

· You live and die—that's it.

Do you want to stop believing in and living according to loser principles and start living the SHE life God has in store for you? Wanna start following God's instruction book for life? Wanna find forgiveness for the ways you've messed up and get wisdom and determination for doing it right from this point on?

Don't cheat yourself out of the good things that are waiting for you any longer. Don't cheat yourself out of the abundant life God promises you (see John 10:10). Now is the time to get into the game—to step into the role God designed for you to play in his eternal plan! So take the time to study God's road map, commit to doing life his way, and make choices that will honor him. In the process you'll find yourself becoming

a SAFE girl
a HEALTHY girl
an EMPOWERED girl

REBECCA
SAYS

Whenever we've broken God's rules, we need to go to God, confess our sin, and ask his forgiveness to know we have been set free from our past. One thing we need to remember when it comes to God's rules is that they are given to us for our good—not to limit our fun. Living by God's road map makes us secure in his care.

I grew up in a large family, the oldest of seven kids. As a young girl, I remember my mum teaching me how to wrap my baby brothers tightly in a blanket and then hold them with strong arms so that they would feel safe. Within the boundaries of that blanket in my arms, they knew they were secure. I think this also applies to us.

When we are held within our Creator's loving arms and living according to his plan for us, we experience security, peace, and joy.

THE BUZZ ON A BIBLE SHE

THE SAMARITAN WOMAN

STATUS:	Had lived with five different men
RULE-BUSTING BEHAVIOR:	Sexual impurity
WHY SHE WASN'T PART OF THE IN CROWD:	First, she was a Samaritan (a race looked down on by the Jews). Second, she was a woman, and women were not highly esteemed in those days—until Jesus came and changed all that. Third, well, let's just say she didn't have a squeaky-clean rep.
A "CHANCE" ENCOUNTER:	She met Jesus unexpectedly one day by a well. She'd gone there to get some water as she always did, but this day was different. Jesus had gone out of his way to offer her the SHE life.
EAVESDROPPING ON THEIR CONVERSATION:	S. W.: You are a Jew, and I am a Samaritan woman. Why are you asking me for a drink? Jesus: If you only knew the gift God has for you and who I am, you would ask me, and I would give you living water. S. W.: Where would you get this living water? Jesus: People soon become thirsty again after drinking this water. But the water I give them takes away thirst altogether. It becomes a perpetual spring within them, giving them eternal life. S. W.: Please, sir . . . give me some of that water! Then I'll never be thirsty again.
WHO IS THIS GUY?	Jesus asked about the rules she'd broken. Amazed that Jesus knew her life story, the Samaritan woman didn't feel angry or condemned by his words. Instead, she saw the love and mercy Jesus offered her that she'd never seen before and certainly didn't deserve.
A NEW SET OF RULES:	The Bible says SHE left her water pot beside the well and went back to the village and told everyone what Jesus had done.
WANT MORE DETAILS?	For the whole scoop, check out John 4:1-30.

REBECCA SAYS

WHAT IS HEALTHY?

When I think of healthy, I think of my goddaughter, Lexi Rivers. Her parents adopted her from China, and she is such a joy to them and everyone she meets. Now, at two years old, she toddles around with a healthy flush in her cheeks, full of life and energy, and I see the picture of what we can be when we're living according to God's plan for us as his young SHE women.

REBECCA SAYS

WHAT IS SAFE?

I learned the meaning of safety from a little girl in Ecuador. It all started when my brother Joel and I went on a trip to meet the child he sponsors through Compassion International. We visited the smiling Compassion children in remote villages, serving food at one of the projects and singing worship songs with them. In one classroom, my attention was drawn to a little girl about eight years old. A large, blanketed lump covered almost half of her small body. With her permission, I looked under the blankets and discovered the tiny face of a baby who was only weeks old. At the intrusion into her safe little haven and the awakening by cold air and a strange face, the baby started to cry. The girl (whom I later found out was the infant's cousin) quickly took the child back to its mother. It hit me that I too long to be protected, cocooned in love, and tucked away from danger.

REBECCA SAYS

WHAT IS EMPOWERED?

On a family vacation years ago, I learned to windsurf. We were staying on the lovely Sunshine Coast in Queensland, Australia. The weather was beautiful, the beach was just a few minutes' walk away, and the sparkling lake beckoned me. I was determined to conquer the Windsurfer and not let it conquer me. So after a few lessons from the instructor, I gave it a go. I lost my balance a few times, but eventually I found myself sailing solo across the water, feeling the exhilaration of being powered and propelled by the wind. The windsurfing thing required some serious concentration for a novice like me. But even an experienced windsurfer would say that to really go places, to be fully powered by the wind, you have to listen to instructions, apply strong concentration, and put consistent effort into it. Just as in the rest of life, you have to give it all you've got.

9 SECRETS TO A WHOLE NEW **SHE!**

SAFE

SHE is secure.

SHE is connected.

SHE is feminine.

HEALTHY

SHE is beautiful.

SHE is pure.

SHE is free.

EMPOWERED

SHE is guided.

SHE is boundaried.

SHE is purposeful.

Don't just read this book. Let it change your life for good. Make it stick to your life where it applies. You may find that it's not your family or friend who is keeping you from changing, but you and only you. Take baby-change steps. They add up and make a huge difference. But we promise, once you make the change to be a God-ruled SHE, you won't want to go back. You won't want to return to the UNSAFE, UNHEALTHY, UNEMPOWERED—and not-pleasing-to-God—she you used to be.

SO... WHATCHA GONNA DO?

You can't obey God's instructions on your own. Your SHE journey begins with an intimate relationship with Jesus. And as with the Samaritan woman, it means meeting Jesus right where you are:

1 Ask him to forgive the sins you've committed and invite him to come and rule your heart.

2 Ask the Holy Spirit to guide you every day forward for every decision you make.

3 With the Holy Spirit's help, stick to the guidelines you make for your life and don't turn back.

4 Celebrate your safe, healthy, and empowered life to come. Then enjoy!

If you made this decision to walk with Jesus for the first time, congratulations! This is a day to celebrate! Sign and date below so you will always remember the anniversary of your relationship with Jesus.

If you've been taking a bad detour and you decided to recommit to walking with Christ today, congratulations! Sign and date below so you'll always remember this important day of your spiritual journey.

....
Name

....
Date

SHEism: **SHE** is Safe, Healthy, and Empowered because **SHE** is God-ruled!

SHE IS SECURE

FIND PHYSICAL AND EMOTIONAL SAFETY THROUGH CHRIST.

*In peace I will lie down and sleep, for you
alone, O LORD, will keep me safe.*

Psalm 4:8

It was an ordinary Sunday evening on February 1, 2004, in Sarasota, Florida. Carlie Brucia, a student at McIntosh Middle School, left her friend's house and headed home, but she never made it.

The next day, surveillance cameras from Evie's Car Wash were routinely examined. One of the tapes showed a backpack-toting Carlie, who had apparently taken a shortcut home through the closed car-wash parking lot. At approximately 6:20 p.m., a man approached Carlie. After speaking for a few seconds to a non-resisting, bewildered-looking Carlie, the man took her by the forearm and led her away. Carlie's dead body was found five days later near a Sarasota church.

WHAT ABOUT YOU?

What would you have done if you'd been in Carlie's position?

1. Would you have stopped to talk to the man?

2. Would you have tried to be nice to the man?

3. Would you have refused to talk to the man and bolted in the other direction?

4. Would you have screamed and immediately drawn attention to the situation?

5. Would you have done something else?

> *Even when you are chased by those who seek to kill you, your life is safe in the care of the LORD your God, secure in his treasure pouch!*
>
> *1 Samuel 25:29*

FASTEN YOUR SAFETY BELT

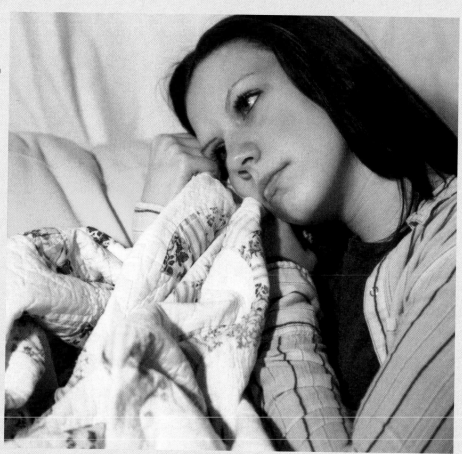

Unfortunately, tragedies such as Carlie's are not all that rare. You've seen Amber Alert signs mounted above the highway, alerting motorists to missing children they should look out for. You've heard about abuse nightmares described by your friends.

Maybe you've experienced dangerous near misses yourself. Perhaps someone left you, betrayed you, died, let you down, or failed to protect you as he or she should have. Now you're left with nagging feelings of fear and insecurity.

Before you can truly develop into the total person God designed you to be, you have to take care of the basics—food, water, oxygen, sleep. But staying safe is about more than just your body. SHEs have a security system to protect their whole self—body, emotions, and soul.

Mark out a straight path for your feet; stay on the safe path. Proverbs 4:26

SECURITY CHECKPOINT

1. Have you ever depended on some-one—or something—who let you down or failed to keep you safe?

   Yes　　　　No

2. Do you feel as if an important person in your life should have done his or her job better?

   Yes　　　　No

3. Do you feel as if someone in your life who should have stuck around is now gone?

   Yes　　　　No

4. Has someone's lie hurt you?

   Yes　　　　No

5. Do you find it hard to trust because of the number of people who have left or disappointed you?

   Yes　　　　No

6. Have feelings of insecurity kept you from enjoying life and being yourself?

   Yes　　　　No

7. Do you feel alone, unprotected, and unable to keep yourself safe?

   Yes　　　　No

8. Have you experienced hurts from a father or mother (through physical, mental, or emotional abuse or absence)?

   Yes　　　　No

9. Have you ever felt wounded by a friend (who gave you false advice or no advice at all)?

   Yes　　　　No

10. Have you ever felt abandoned by your church or your pastor (through failure to effectively lead and guard)?

    Yes　　　　No

11. Have you ever felt deceived by culture (for misleading you about your identity as a woman)?

    Yes　　　　No

12. Have you ever felt disappointed by God (who appeared to let you down)?

    Yes　　　　No

REBECCA SAYS

I went into full-time ministry at the age of 16, and since then writing, recording, touring, and performing have been my life. I'm on the road eight or nine months of the year, performing up to two hundred shows, conducting interviews, and adjusting constantly to new faces and places.

In the fall of 1999, after finishing a grueling 13-month tour, I decided to fulfill a lifelong dream and go on a short-term mission trip to Romania. For two months, I handed out sandwiches to street kids, played with children at the girls' home, cleaned, prayed, and did all I could to pour love into their lives. Though the trip was great, it wasn't until afterward that I felt the toll that both the yearlong tour and the mission trip had taken on me.

I returned to Nashville feeling disoriented, emotionally vulnerable, and completely spent. Something was wrong inside me, but I didn't know how to fix it.

My first instinct was to run away and somehow try to escape the inner turmoil. So partly to clear my head and partly because of society's pressure to be independent, I moved out of my family home and into a tiny house in a quaint downtown section of Franklin, Tennessee. A little haven . . . but it was not to be.

I experienced the most horrible time of my life in the quietness of that isolation. I'd come "home" after a stressful day in the studio to find no one to talk to, no one to care. I grew desperately lonely.

I felt my heart go into self-protection mode. To cope with the pain, I began to shut off from other people and shut down. Feeling like I was going crazy, I shared my situation and pain with my pastor. One of the wise things he said that day was, "Rebecca, is God trustworthy? Then trust him."

It's amazing how we can overlook such simple truths until we really need them. The power of "God is trustworthy, so trust him" was like flipping on a switch and shining a beacon of light on me. I finally understood how much I'd been relying on myself, trying to be strong and independent, instead of leaning on God for strength and finding my identity and protection in him. I saw that I had pulled away from the security of family and the support of godly friends and lost out because of it.

Through my experience, I learned much about the power and importance of community, that we're made to rely on each other and not be lone rangers. And I realized that many of us women at some point experience the agony of feeling lonely and unprotected.

Turn your ear to listen to me; rescue me quickly. Be my rock of protection, a fortress where I will be safe.
Psalm 31:2

All who listen to me will live in peace,
untroubled by fear of harm.
Proverbs 1:33

DANGER ZONE QUIZ

1 When you hear about bad things that could happen to you, what do you do?

a) Get really afraid and shut down emotionally.

b) Refuse to do anything or go anywhere where I might get hurt.

c) Decide I can't do anything to stop bad things from happening, so I throw all caution to the wind and live dangerously.

d) Find out what I can do to stay the most safe in certain areas and do those things, then go about living my life.

2 When something bad happens to you, how do you respond?

a) Blame myself and decide I had it coming or that I brought it on myself.

b) Place the blame on other people or on God.

c) Learn from the negative situation and figure out what I could do differently next time to avoid the danger.

d) Become bitter and shut myself off from everyone, deciding no one is trustworthy.

3 When you sense danger to yourself, what do you do?

a) Respond to my gut feeling and get away from the person or situation.

b) Go back and forth indecisively as I try to avoid hurting someone else's feelings.

c) Ignore my feelings about the sense of danger and forge ahead.

d) Become so crippled by my fears that I can't think straight.

You probably noticed that the answers show a few different approaches to personal safety. One girl may take every warning so seriously that she ends up living in fear and can't do anything without worrying about it. Another may fail to take responsibility, ignoring danger signals or blaming others for her situations. Try to aim for a third approach: avoid extremes. Don't let fear run your life or paralyze you, but don't cast caution to the wind either. But *do* learn from your own experiences and from hearing about the mistakes of others! Don't put yourself into dangerous situations or ignore warning signals, but remember to trust in God to keep you safe by letting you know how to do the smart thing in frightening situations.

DID YA KNOW...

PHYSICAL SECURITY:

WHAT YOU SHOULD KNOW

- One out of every three women murdered in the United States is killed by a husband or boyfriend.[1]
- According to the FBI, 20 percent of female homicide victims are between 15 and 24 years old.[2]
- Sixty-one percent of all rape victims are younger than 18.[3]
- About one American woman in six is raped in her lifetime.[4]

DATING SECURITY:

WHAT YOU SHOULD KNOW

- Twenty percent of high school girls have been physically or sexually assaulted by someone they were dating.[5]
- About one in 11 girls reported having broken up with a boyfriend because she was afraid he would physically harm her.[6]
- Studies show that 67 percent of young women reporting rape were raped in dating situations.[7]

COMPUTER SECURITY:

WHAT YOU SHOULD KNOW

- One in five people under 18 who use computer chat rooms has been approached over the Internet by pedophiles.[8] *(Quick 411: A pedophile is a creepy adult who takes advantage of kids and teens sexually.)*
- Eighty-nine percent of sexual solicitations are made either in chat rooms or through instant messages.[9] *(Quick 411: A sexual solicitation is a lure or a trap where a creepy adult tries to take advantage of someone sexually.)*

YOU SAID IT

TOP 4 SAFE PLACES

1. Home
2. Church
3. Youth group
4. School

TOP 8 SAFE PEOPLE

1. Parents
2. Grandparents
3. Friends
4. Boyfriend
5. Sister
6. Teacher
7. Pastor
8. Myself

According to a recent
SHE survey of 2,000 girls

SHE SPEAKS

KAYLA (14)

I felt most unsafe when I had a close friend of mine completely betray me. Then she brought other people to my door to join in verbal attacks against me. I just stood there in my doorway and took it all. Finally, I came inside and cried and cried.

DESIREE (17)

When I was in ninth grade, I got into a group of kids who were heading down a destructive path in life—sex, drugs, and alcohol. Every time we got together, someone would end up getting hurt, and then it was awkward for the rest of us because we didn't know what to do or where to go. It really pulled me away from my parents, and even today I can't be open with them about where I'm going, even though it isn't anywhere bad anymore.

BROOKE (17)

I felt really unsafe once when I was waiting for a bus and a man kept bothering me, trying to talk to me. He then parked his car, got out, and tried to keep talking to me. I looked for his license plate, but he didn't have any. He had gotten really close to me—then the bus came.

Fearing people is a dangerous trap, but trusting the LORD means safety.
Proverbs 29:25

HOLY BODYGUARD

GOD'S PART OF THE DEAL

WHAT IF I GO SOMEWHERE WHERE I FEEL UNSAFE?

The LORD keeps watch over you as you come and go.

Psalm 121:8

WHAT IF I'M PEE-MY-PANTS SCARED?

[Jesus says:] "I am leaving you with a gift—peace of mind and heart."

John 14:27

WHAT IF I DON'T HAVE A SAFE PLACE TO GO?

You are my strength; I wait for you to rescue me, for you, O God, are my fortress.

Psalm 59:9

WHAT IF I FEEL AS IF EVERYTHING IN MY LIFE IS FALLING APART?

[He says:] "I am the LORD, and I do not change."

Malachi 3:6

WHAT IF I FEEL TOO WEAK TO PROTECT MYSELF?

God is our refuge and strength, always ready to help in times of trouble.

Psalm 46:1

Now let's get something straight. God *does* promise to protect us. But that doesn't mean we should surgically remove the commonsense compartment of our brain! (After all, he's the one who gave it to us.) And it doesn't mean we should ignore the smart people he's put in our life.

Without wise leadership, a nation falls; there is safety in having many advisers.

Proverbs 11:14

SHE GETS PERSONAL

Where do you feel the most safe?

When have you felt really unsafe, and what did you do?

Who makes you feel unsafe?

How do you usually handle scary situations?

YEAH, BUT . . .

- I don't want to be paranoid about danger.
- Life is no fun without risks.
- God will take care of me. I don't have to do anything else.
- Other: _____

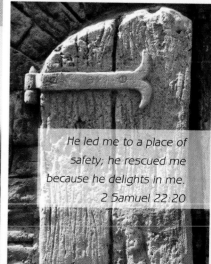

He led me to a place of safety; he rescued me because he delights in me.

2 Samuel 22:20

SHE IS SECURE

Those who fear the LORD are secure. Proverbs 14:26

PAGE 25

THE LIE: I WILL ALWAYS BE AFRAID.

THE TRUTH: GOD PROMISES TO KEEP HIS KIDS SAFE.

SO WHAT'S UP
WITH THE KNEE-KNOCKING,
LIP-QUIVERING,
PIT-IN-THE-STOMACH
FEAR
WE ALL FACE?

SOMETIMES WE DON'T KNOW THE PROMISES.

Do you feel clueless about what God's promises are? When you don't know what he says, it's like having a $1,000 check sitting in a drawer but never cashing it. All the insights you will ever need in your whole life are found in the Bible. Learn them and cash in on the promises.

SOMETIMES WE DON'T ASK.

Do you ever talk to your friends, parents, or church leaders before you talk to God about something that is causing you concern? Maybe you keep it all bottled up inside and don't tell anyone about it. God knows about every one of your fears, but he wants you to talk with him about them as you would go to a good father or a close friend or a wise counselor.

SOMETIMES WE DON'T TRUST.

Has an important person in your life broken his or her promises? That person has lied, so it's hard for you to believe that Someone we can't see will keep his word. But even if everyone else lets us down, God never will. He has never broken one promise. Ever. And he's not about to start now.

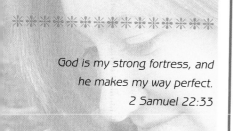

✳✳✳✳✳✳✳✳✳✳✳✳✳✳✳

God is my strong fortress, and he makes my way perfect.
2 Samuel 22:33

SHE SPEAKS

ASHLEY (19)

I felt very unsafe walking home from school late at night. I live over a mile from my college. I felt physically unsafe. But then I remembered that the Bible promises that God hasn't given us a spirit of fear, but of power and love and sound mind (see 2 Timothy 1:7). So I began to pray. I prayed all the way home and got there safely. I called my mom and asked her to buy me some pepper spray.

SHE SPEAKS

BRIANNA (16)

Sometimes I feel unsafe when I am driving alone at night through unfamiliar neighborhoods—like ones on the wrong side of town. But whenever I am afraid, God always leads me to sing praise songs to him. That calms me down and comforts me.

SHE SPEAKS

TAMARA (17)

Coming from a Middle Eastern background, I have always been complimented on my olive skin and dark hair. My parents, both born in Iraq, immigrated to America to explore the possibilities of life in a free country. I never viewed my cultural background as a handicap, but rather I embraced it.

Then September 11, 2001, happened, and my outlook on my background changed. One day while my sister and I were in the dressing room of a department store, a couple of teenage girls threatened us. My security and protection were gone as I feared that people would associate me and my family with terrorists.

Then I read Psalm 27:1 (NIV): "The LORD is my light and my salvation—whom shall I fear? The LORD is the stronghold of my life—of whom shall I be afraid?" As I read this verse, I realized how David must have felt as he fled for his life from King Saul. Throughout everything, David trusted God for his protection. In the same way, God was with me through both September 11 and the war in Iraq. Since God was on my side, I did not need to fear man. And as I enter college soon, I know God will remain my protector.

3 FEAR-BUSTING TIPS
. . . to transform you from a knee-knocker to a security seeker!

1 Choose a verse about safety from this chapter or from the index in your Bible. Write it down and put it in your locker or your notebook. Memorize it and say it to yourself when you feel afraid.

2 Find a peaceful place to sit and be quiet with God. Talk to him about everything that is on your heart. Tell him about your fears. Tell him about the ways you've been let down. Tell him how much you want him to help you. Tell him about the verse you found about being safe, and pray his words back to him. Then sit quietly and let him comfort you and fill you with new strength.

3 Go about your day confidently. You can trust God to see to the needs you've asked him for. And when things get really scary again, thank him for being your protector.

God has said, "I will never fail you. I will never abandon you."
Hebrews 13:5

SHE GETS PERSONAL

Are you facing an unsafe situation right now? an unhealthy relationship? a habit that is harmful to your body? an environment that is stunting your spiritual growth? emotional or physical abuse?

YES   NO

IF YOU CIRCLED YES, read Hebrews 13:5 (in column at left). Then write down this sentence in your journal, tape it to your car dashboard, or hang it on the bathroom mirror:

"Jesus, thank you that you will not leave me alone to handle _____."

It's true—God doesn't want you to face this alone. He promises to be with you. *And* he gives you people to help you face this tough situation. Your next step: Find an adult you trust who walks with God and ask her for help. Do it today.

IF YOU CIRCLED NO, read this: If you are not facing an unsafe situation right now, you can be sure you will sometime in the future. Look up and read the second half of Hebrews 13:5 in your Bible. Then write down this sentence in your journal, tape it to your car dashboard, or hang it on the bathroom mirror: "Jesus, no matter what lies ahead, thank you that you will not leave me alone." Your next step: Find a trusted adult who walks with God and ask her in advance if you can come to her for help. When you find yourself in an unsafe situation in the future, you'll know she's there for you.

The LORD is my fortress, protecting me from danger.
Psalm 27:1

A CRASH COURSE
IN SELF-DEFENSE

YOUR PART OF THE DEAL

THE LIE:	I'M POWERLESS TO PROTECT MYSELF.
THE TRUTH:	GOD GIVES US WISDOM TO STAY AWAY FROM DANGER.

Those who trust their own insight are foolish, but anyone who walks in wisdom is safe.
Proverbs 28:26

No matter how many tae kwon do lessons we take, we can't rely only on ourselves for protection. We need God and we need other people. But God does want us to be active participants in our own safety.

God promised the prophet Elijah he would speak to him on Mount Sinai (often called the mountain of God). Maybe Elijah was expecting God to show up in the big stuff—the windstorm, the earthquake, the fire. But God didn't speak through any of those things. Instead, he chose to speak to Elijah in a gentle whisper (see 1 Kings 19:11-12). And guess what? He still speaks to us that way today.

That still, small voice goes by different names—intuition, a gut feeling, an internal security system—but whatever you call it, it's part of God's design for our self-protection. While we can't control how others behave, we can be wise in our interactions with them. Sometimes we get confused between genuine Christian love and just being nice. Being nice—but not wise—can put us in some awkward and unsafe positions. That's when we need to listen to what God is saying to us. Sometimes we need to put the niceties aside and call the shots.

SHE SPEAKS

MIKKELLE (18)

Recently a coworker at my job asked me to give him a ride somewhere after work. I don't know him very well, and honestly just his being a guy made me feel uneasy. He kept badgering me to give him a ride home. Finally I called my mom, acting as if she had called me. I told him I had to leave right away to get home. This helped me avoid the situation altogether.

JESSICA (16)

I was out late at night driving with some of my friends. We ended up in a deserted part of town. My friends started running around and making a lot of noise. Though we weren't doing anything illegal, I had an uneasy feeling—so much so that my friends thought I was sick. I asked them to take me home and they did. I guess I won't ever know why I was so anxious and uneasy over something so small, but I was glad to get home.

GIRL TALK!

Along with a friend, read the following and decide whether they are true or false:

1. (T/F) You can't control how others around you behave, but you can learn how to use your mind, voice, and body to help keep you safe.
2. (T/F) Being polite is always the best way to deal with a person who is behaving badly.
3. (T/F) It's your fault if you are hurt, tricked, or betrayed.
4. (T/F) You are responsible for what boundaries are comfortable or acceptable for you.
5. (T/F) It's not your job to make other people feel happy, loved, attractive, or secure.
6. (T/F) You should never be forced to be touched by anyone else. It's your choice.
7. (T/F) You do not have a say over who enters your personal space.
8. (T/F) It's always acceptable to say "Stop!" "Wait!" or "No!"
9. (T/F) You are entitled to call someone to help you out if you're feeling unsafe.
10. (T/F) You can trust your instincts about what is going on around you.

CHECK YOUR ANSWERS:

1. T; 2. F; 3. F; 4. T; 5. T; 6. T; 7. F; 8. T; 9. T; 10. T

Do your answers match up? If you came up with different answers to any of the questions, look at the questions again. Discuss them with a friend, and if you're confused, talk with a mentor or a trusted adult.

SHE'S BEEN THERE

8 WAYS TO TELL IF HE MEANS TROUBLE

Sit with a trusted, godly woman (such as your mom, your grandma, a family friend, or your youth pastor). Talk about the following clues you can watch for in a guy you know—or will know—that could tell you if he is a safety hazard. Ask this woman for her own stories from her dating days, and talk about some of the guys you know.

Check any of the boxes that apply to your situation.

○ Can be bossy and controlling
○ Gets easily jealous of the time you spend with your friends and other people
○ Tries to dictate what you do, wear, and think, and how you spend your time
○ Treats women poorly and says degrading things about them
○ Puts you down or makes fun of you
○ Drinks or uses drugs
○ Is physically violent
○ Pressures you to have sex

FAQs FREQUENTLY ASKED QUESTIONS
HOW CAN I PROTECT MYSELF FROM BEING RAPED?

1. ALWAYS walk with other people or let someone know where you'll be.

2. ALWAYS walk quickly, purposefully, and with an air of confidence.

3. ALWAYS be aware of your surroundings. Before you leave a building or a car, look around and see how well lit the area is. Are other people around? What is the most direct route to your destination?

4. ALWAYS keep your car and house doors and windows locked.

5. NEVER associate with strangers, even ones you met an hour or two before and had a conversation with. Never leave a party with someone you just met that evening.

6. NEVER accept drinks from anyone you don't know. Drinks can be laced with date-rape drugs that cause a woman to become unconscious and allow an attack.

7. NEVER use drugs or alcohol—they slow down your reaction time and make you more vulnerable.

8. NEVER get into situations or places that make you feel uncomfortable or confused.

Quote Me!
Practice these power phrases that help you stay safe:

- "I DON'T WANT TO BE HUGGED RIGHT NOW."
- "I DON'T LIKE THAT."
- "I DON'T WANT TO DO THAT."
- "THAT HURTS."
- "THAT'S NOT FUNNY."
- "STOP THAT!"

SHE ASKS

GABRIELLE (18)
I have struggled with serious depression for seven years and have spent more than a year in different hospitals and treatment centers. I regret that I have tried to kill myself a few times, and I have been a cutter since I was in eighth grade. I am now a senior, and I was doing really well for a while. Then in February of this year, I got sick again. I started cutting, and I felt suicidal. From my experiences before, I knew what could happen, so I checked myself into the mental-health unit at a nearby hospital. Am I the only one who goes through stuff like this?

> If you want to live securely in the land, follow my decrees and obey my regulations.
> Leviticus 25:18

SHE ASKS

MEAGAN (14)
What worries you most about being famous? How do you deal with the stuff you're afraid about?

> The name of the LORD is a strong fortress; the godly run to him and are safe.
> Proverbs 18:10

REBECCA SAYS

At times in my life, I have also battled serious mind assault, struggling with negative thoughts, fears, and hurts that Satan would like to use to make me live a defeated life. On these kinds of days, I have shared my struggle with my mentor, my mum, or my best friend. Each time she encourages me to reject what is not true, replace it with biblical truth, and pray against further attack. I have learned through these experiences that I cannot allow these harmful thoughts to start spinning around in my head. If I do, they can grow and become a deadly tornado, causing all kinds of damage.

....

One of the downsides of life in the spotlight is that some unusual people with very strange ideas follow me around—some might call them stalkers. I've even had guys I don't know tell me God has told them that they are *the one* for me. The scariest situation I've encountered was when a guy threatened to kill me if I became romantically involved with someone else besides him. There were definitely some fearful thoughts attacking me at that time. What comforted me was knowing that if my life were to be taken, I would be with my best friend, Jesus, face-to-face. For believers, "to live is Christ and to die is gain" (Philippians 1:21, NIV).

SHE SPEAKS

KRISTEN (15)

The time I felt most unsafe was when my dad started screaming at me and slammed me up against the wall. I left the house after that, and following a few failed attempts to get him to apologize, I have not talked to him since.

SHE SPEAKS

SARAH (13)

The last time I felt unsafe was just a few weeks ago. I was taking my puppy for a walk in the development where I live. There were no streetlights around. I felt vulnerable.

SHE SPEAKS

EMILY (17)

Toward the end of the relationship with my last boyfriend, I felt very emotionally unsafe. I constantly felt like I was being used, and during my time with him, I distanced myself from God and his plan for my life. I'm usually happy and agreeable, and my change in behavior was noticed by many people in my life. I eventually broke up with the guy, and after taking a long time to get over him, I am now getting back to being close to God. I am letting God back in to fill my loneliness.

FAQs FREQUENTLY ASKED QUESTIONS

WHAT IS DATING VIOLENCE?

Dating violence: Repeated pattern of actual or threatened acts that emotionally, verbally, physically, or sexually hurt another person.

WHAT IS EMOTIONAL ABUSE?

Emotional abuse: Jealousy and possessiveness, which lead to accusations and interrogations. You become scared to do anything that might set the other person off. You begin to doubt yourself. You are kept isolated. Your independence and confidence in yourself are destroyed.

WHAT IS PHYSICAL ABUSE?

Physical abuse: Pushing, hitting, slapping, and kicking.

WHAT IS SEXUAL ABUSE?

Sexual abuse: Being mistreated through sexual acts, demands, or insults.

NEED HELP?
Do you need help right now?
Are you experiencing abuse from a boyfriend or a parent?
CALL THE NATIONAL DOMESTIC VIOLENCE HOTLINE
800-799-7233

More Safety Tips

- GET AWAY!
- USE YOUR VOICE!
- USE YOUR MIND. (Ask yourself calmly, *What can I do?*)
- BLOCK, HIT, AND KICK.
- TRUST YOUR GUT. (Listen when your body tells you something is wrong.)
- TELL! (Don't let things continue or get worse by not telling important people about what happened to you.)
- SCREAM FIRST; ask questions later.
- TAKE A SELF-DEFENSE COURSE offered in your community. (Check with your school or YWCA for locations.)

THE BUZZ ON A BIBLE SHE

HAGAR

STATUS:	Sarai's servant. She'd worked for her boss Sarai for many years. She must have heard Abram and Sarai talk about God's promise to give them a son in their childless old age. She must have witnessed their discouragement as the years passed without seeing the promise fulfilled, and the only thing born to Abram and Sarai were new aches and pains in their 90- and 80-year-old bodies.
OUTTA NOWHERE:	Sarai decided to help God out. She told Hagar to sleep with Abram and to give him a son. As always, Hagar obeyed. After all, they were her protectors. She depended on them. She could trust them to know what was best for her, couldn't she? (Obviously not.)
ATTACK OF THE GREEN-EYED MONSTER:	Hagar became pregnant, and Sarai got jealous. Through one incident, Hagar's security and shelter were gone, replaced with suffering and rejection from someone she'd likely trusted for years. Not even the law took care of her. It prevented Abram from stepping in and shielding Hagar from Sarai's wrath without Sarai's permission. And Sarai certainly wasn't going to give that!
SPRINT TO SAFETY:	Hagar fled to the only safe place she knew—the desert.
HER SURPRISE VISITOR:	An angel found her there and called her by name. God met Hagar in her unprotected place.
HE SAID:	The angel of the Lord found Hagar beside a desert spring. The angel said to her, "Hagar, Sarai's servant, where have you come from, and where are you going?" (Genesis 16:8). God knew Hagar's past and what she'd been through. He found and cared for her in her present situation. And he looked forward with her to her future and told her what she needed to do to move on.
SHE SAID:	"You are the God who sees me." Hagar became convinced of God's love for her.
WANT MORE DETAILS?	For the whole scoop, check out Genesis 16.

DATING BILL OF RIGHTS

- I have the right to be treated with respect.
- I have the right not to be abused—physically, emotionally, or sexually.
- I have the right to say no and be heard.
- I have the right to express my own opinions.
- I have the right to private time and my own space.
- I have the right to have my needs considered as much as my boyfriend's.
- I have the right to have friends of my own.
- I have the right to pursue my own special interests—and not be criticized for pursuing them.
- I have the right to accept a gift without having to give anything in return.
- I have the right to hear about my strengths and assets.
- I have the right to ask others for help if I need it.
- I have the right to live a violence-free life.
- I have the right to change my mind—to "fall out of love" and live with no threats.[10]

MY PERSONAL SAFETY PLAN

Tip: Cut this section out and keep it in your purse, or copy this information onto a note card and keep it in your purse.

1 Get a cell phone. Be sure it's always charged.
2 Always have someone who will pick you up at any time, no questions asked.

Name: _____ Phone #: _____

3 Decide on safe places you can go in case you can't get home.

Safe Place #1: _____

Safe Place #2: _____

Safe Place #3: _____

4 List people you can go to in emergencies.

Name: _____ Phone #: _____

Name: _____ Phone #: _____

Name: _____ Phone #: _____

5 Have an emergency kit with you at all times (spare keys, cash, phone numbers, cell phone, this page, etc.).
6 Establish a safety net of people who will look out for you. Be sure to tell them where you'll be and who you'll be with.

Name: _____

Name: _____

Name: _____

GiRL TALK!

Read about some of the situations some of the girls in our SHE survey found themselves in and discuss them with a friend.

IF YOU WERE IN THEIR FLIP-FLOPS, WHAT WOULD YOU DO?

HANNAH (16)

In my school, the band director often made me and my friends slightly uncomfortable. Sometimes he would give us shoulder massages. His all-around presence made us uncomfortable to be alone with him. Personally, I was never very nice to him—sometimes even hostile and disrespectful. I really wanted to quit band because of him and other reasons.

CARLEY (17)

I was a freshman in high school, sitting in political-science class near the wall. This boy kept trying to put his hand down my pants, and I kept moving forward. Yet he didn't get the idea and reached over and kept harassing me. In the hallway, he tried to squeeze my chest. I told the teacher and administration about it, but they ignored my plea and said I was overreacting.

GRETCHEN (15)

My stepdad has a messed-up way of communicating—he doesn't until he loses it! He spazzed out one day because my sister and I were making too much noise opening and closing the doors. He came in my room and kicked me on the leg. It wasn't even hard enough to make me say "ouch," but I was shocked into speechlessness that he would do that at all. I just cried and prayed.

 SHEism: A truly protected SHE finds her protection through God and the wisdom he provides.

SHE IS CONNECTED

FIND SAFETY THROUGH INTIMACY WITH GOD AND INTIMACY WITH PEOPLE.

The LORD is close to all who call on him,
yes, to all who call on him in truth.
Psalm 145:18

YOU MAY HAVE HEARD ABOUT TAMAGOTCHI VIRTUAL PETS . . . BUT DID YOU KNOW THERE ARE NOW VIRTUAL GIRLFRIENDS?

That's right, now guys can have it all—the connection and thrill of having a significant other without the strings attached . . . and without the possibility of getting hurt. All they have to do is download their artificial girlfriend onto their 3G phone and presto! They now have a techno-girl to send messages to, flirt with, and buy gifts for (using real money!).[1]

That may sound a little over the top, but aren't we all at least a little guilty of looking for virtual relationships? Maybe we don't go to the extreme of downloading artificial friends or siblings or boyfriends. But part of us wants the intimacy without the risk, the connection without the commitment.

But God says there's a better way. We'll never be fulfilled unless we have meaningful connections with him and with the important people in our life.

SHE ASKS

MEAGAN (14)

What's it like to be on the road, away from your friends, so much? Do you ever get lonely?

REBECCA SAYS

Life on the road has made friendships and relationships more difficult because I'm away from home—and normal life—so much. I have to be very proactive in reaching out and in maintaining my friendships. Simple thoughtfulness means a lot to my friends—sending a postcard, making a phone call, writing an e-mail, going out for coffee while I'm in town. One of God's biggest gifts to me has been my best friend, Karleen. I prayed for two years that God would provide a strong Christian friend to laugh and cry with . . . one who would share a bond of faith. Karleen is now married and has four kids, and even though our lives are so different, God has connected us deeply. Countless times I have shared something I'm going through with her, and she has told me how she has been learning the same thing through a completely different set of circumstances. God blesses the friendships where he has been invited to be at the center.

HEY! Are You Ready to Take the INTIMACY CHALLENGE?

BEFORE THE INTIMACY CHALLENGE	AFTER THE INTIMACY CHALLENGE
Shallow relationships	Meaningful relationships
Surface-level friendships	Gut-level honesty
Share only one thing with family: your address	Healthy interactions with family
Get burned in relationships with guys	Healthy intimacy with guys
Sunday-only appointments with God	Fuller knowledge of God

INTIMACY CHECKPOINT

- [ ] Do you resist getting close to others for fear of being hurt?
- [ ] Do you mistrust God because of the ways people have let you down?
- [ ] Do you feel that no one understands the real you?
- [ ] Do you often fight feelings of loneliness?
- [ ] Is intimacy a foreign concept to you?
- [ ] Do you find that you fill your need for intimacy through unsafe outlets?

The Lord is a friend to those who fear him.
Psalm 25:14

FAQs FREQUENTLY ASKED QUESTIONS
WHAT IS INTIMACY?

- INTIMACY   the ability to connect deeply with someone

- INTIMACY   possible with God as well as with people

- INTIMACY   something we're all created to desire

INTIMACY TESTS

width—it grows through many shared talks and activities that are part of a friendship

length—it develops over a sustained period or season of life

depth—it engages the deepest parts of who we are and reveals our thoughts, faults, shortcomings, fears, and shame, as well as our more positive qualities

DID YA **KNOW...**

Three-quarters of adults say that having close personal friendships is a top priority.

Seven out of ten Americans indicate that having a close personal relationship with God is a top priority in their life.[2]

Wherever you go, I will go; wherever you live, I will live. Your people will be my people, and your God will be my God.
Ruth 1:16

SHE ASKS

CHRISTINE (14)

Can I have the same kind of connections with my non-Christian friends that I have with my Christian friends?

REBECCA SAYS

In my life it has been very important to have strong Christian friends. I need the accountability and encouragement they give, and I need to be able to pray and talk openly about my faith with them. Positive peer pressure can have a wonderful impact on our life. Similarly, negative peer pressure is something we must be on our guard against. However, I believe it's important to have friends who don't know God too, so we can show them Jesus' love through our actions.

SHE SPEAKS

AMANDA (AGE UNKNOWN)

I've been through a lot in my life: seven years of sexual abuse at the hands of my father, the death of my grandfather, and the recent death of my best friend. I've been hurt and abandoned by almost everyone who says they care. It's hard, so I struggle with the issue of God's love all the time. When I feel myself getting closer to God in worship, I get so scared and panicked that I have to leave because my life has told me that when you get close to someone you get hurt.

STACY (18)

I haven't been emotionally intimate with anyone. That's probably the reason I went to the physical part of intimacy—sex—with so many guys. If you don't feel emotionally loved, you will go searching for it else-where. We need that [intimacy] so much in our life. That's where I fell. I was looking for love in the wrong places.

YOU SAID IT

TOP 4 RELATIONSHIPS WHERE YOU FIND CONNECTEDNESS

1. Parents
2. Friends
3. Boyfriend
4. Youth Group Leader

OKAY. SO WE KNOW WE NEED INTIMACY. And something inside us *craves* intimacy. But somehow it still slips away from a lot of us. Many of us fail to find that deep, healthy connection with God and with the important people in our life, and we have the hole in our heart to prove it.

Test Your Intimacy IQ

Place a check mark beside each statement that describes you.

COLUMN 1

○ I find it relatively easy to get close to God.

○ I find it pretty easy to get close to other people.

○ I am comfortable depending on others.

○ I am comfortable having other people depend on me.

○ I don't often worry about being abandoned or about someone getting too close to me.

MOST CHECK MARKS IN COLUMN 1:
You are a *receiver* of intimacy. You have a secure style of attachment to other people. You trust people you love and see yourself as worthy of being loved. You find it easy to get close to others and feel comfortable relying on those people. You don't worry about being abandoned or having someone demand too much depth and vulnerability from you. Peers find you confident, likable, and open.

ABBY (14)

Most of my relationships are healthy. I have a strong relationship with my parents, my sisters, my girlfriends, teachers, minister, and even most of my guy friends. Lately I have gotten to be extremely close to my older sister who is 16 (I am 14). I think that part of it is that we're both getting older and more mature. Also, we both share our love for God, who keeps our relationship strong. We're not afraid to tell each other when we mess up. I really enjoy having conversations with her.

COLUMN 2

○ I am somewhat uncomfortable being close to God.

○ I am somewhat uncomfortable being close to others.

○ I find it difficult to trust other people.

○ I find it difficult to allow myself to depend on others.

○ I am nervous when anyone gets too close, and God and others often want me to be more intimate than I feel comfortable being.

MOST CHECK MARKS IN COLUMN 2:
You are a *resister* of intimacy. When someone tries to get close to you, you feel uncomfortable. You find it hard to trust another person completely and don't like to be dependent. You claim not to believe in romantic love or the need for it, which is often a way to make up for deep insecurities. Others often describe you as relatively defensive.

MADISON (17)

I am not a people person. I don't relate to other people because I'm good at different things. Therefore, I don't really have good relationships with boys or girls. I tried having a boyfriend once. I followed my heart instead of my head. I thought it might actually work, but it didn't. It was horrible. Now I'm alone again. And I'm going to stick with listening to my head.

COLUMN 3

○ I find that others are reluctant to get as close as I would like.

○ I often worry that others don't really love me or won't want to stay with me.

○ I often desire to be swallowed up or merged in a relationship with someone.

○ I tend to cause other people to feel smothered.

○ I find that I often scare people away.

MOST CHECK MARKS IN COLUMN 3:
You are a *repeller* of intimacy. You often worry that other people don't really love you and won't stay with you for long. Your desire to get really close sometimes scares other people away. You might find yourself preoccupied with finding "real" love, constantly falling in and out of relationships, but true love has eluded you. As a repeller, you often fail to find true friends, and your confidence fluctuates between extreme highs and lows. Peers could describe you as self-conscious, insecure, and preoccupied with relationship issues.

SHAYNA (15)

I have tried to get close to girls and guys at school and in my youth group, but it hasn't happened. It seems like the harder I try, the further I push them away. They make excuses for not sitting with me or hanging out with me. I struggle with depression anyway, and I can't understand what's so terrible about me that it pushes people away.

So how can you find safe intimacy? We believe that by learning to connect deeply with God, you can learn to connect deeply with others too. In fact, true intimacy cannot happen with other people until you first experience depth with God.

Jonathan made David reaffirm his vow of friendship again, for
Jonathan loved David as he loved himself.
1 Samuel 20:17

THE **GOD** CONNECTION

THE LIE: I can never have an intimate relationship with God.

THE TRUTH: God has been courting you since the day you were born.

YEAH, BUT . . .

- I don't have extra time to spend with God.
- I know I should be spending time with God. I just don't know how.
- I've done too much wrong to find intimacy with God.
- I don't know how to get close to someone I can't see.
- Other: _____

The key to finding that intimacy with God is in spending time with him, every day. You can't just read about it or hear about it—you have to do it yourself. You can't depend on your parents' walk with God or youth pastor's walk with God. You gotta walk it yourself. This is not the kind of thing you check off when you're done—like you might with exercising or washing dishes or going to an appoint-

ment. We're talking about time spent in building a relationship. Becoming God's friend. Sharing everything that is on your heart and listening to what's on his. Falling in love with the one who loves you most. A healthy relationship with God is based on three main things: honesty, trust, and open communication.

HOW CAN I GET INTIMATE WITH GOD?

WIDTH

Make Christ a part of your everyday life.

- Regular prayer. Talk to God when you wake up in the morning. Ask him for help with your math test. Pray with your friend who's going through a breakup.

- Regular Bible reading. Read God's love letter to you in the morning or before you go to sleep.

- Join a small group. Take time to learn with others.

LENGTH

Intimacy with Christ doesn't happen overnight. Just as with your best friend, the longer you develop your relationship with him, the closer you will get to him.

DEPTH

SHEs don't go for fluffy, surface-level Christianity! Let God into the deep parts of you—your thoughts and feelings, your strengths and weaknesses, your sins and successes, your fears and joys. And go beyond the surface with God—search his Word for the deep things he wants to teach you about himself.

SHE SPEAKS

KAITLYN (18)

My dad sexually abused me, so I have never trusted any other man. Though I've been a Christian for a long time, I find it really hard to trust God too.

SHE SPEAKS

NICOLE (16)

God's the only one who understands me completely and is there through thick and thin. I talk to him all the time. He's always there for me, and I can go to him about anything. He is my everything. He loves me for who I am. I spend a lot of time talking to him and reading his Word. I've learned so much in the last couple of years, and he has made me a better person. He forgives me for everything I have done, and he comforts me and is always helping me with the problems I have. It's nice to know that no matter how much everyone will let me down, he never will.

SHE SPEAKS

ANN (16)

My parents always thought that since I went to church and Dad was a pastor, I knew everything in the Christian life. But it was not reinforced at home in my personal life. I've never been intimate with God. That's something I want with God. But I've chosen the wrong path lately. I've fallen so far. It's hard. God's so out of reach. I've pushed him so far away.

SHE SPEAKS

LAUREN (17)

I find that having a personal intimacy with God on a daily basis is absolutely crucial to my Christian life. It doesn't matter what it is—praying before I go to bed, having a small quiet time in the morning before I start my daily routine—just anything that keeps me in touch with God helps im-mensely to keep me on the right track. I find that when I lose touch with God for a few weeks or even just one day, everything about me will change. For one thing, my attitude completely drops. I start to feel more depressed and upset with everything around me. Also, it is so much easier to give in to temptations when I cut myself off from God. I've been struggling a lot with my language and thought life. When I'm constantly in God's Word and practicing a relationship with him, it is really easy to say no to these temptations. But when I fall back from him, I find it hard to do the right thing. And I tend not to care. To me, intimacy with God is almost like a vitamin that I as a Christian need to take every day to be able to live my life the way God intended.

A **SPIRITUAL** CHECKUP

HONESTY

On a scale of 1 to 10, how honest are you with God? (1 = I keep my heart-doors locked; 10 = I spill my guts to him)

1   2   3   4   5   6   7   8   9   10

TATTOO THIS ON YOUR BRAIN:

"My heart has heard you say, 'Come and talk with me.' And my heart responds, 'LORD, I am coming'" (Psalm 27:8).

List five things you find the hardest to be honest with God about. Talk to him about them every day for the next seven days.

....

TRUST

On a scale of 1 to 10, how much do you trust God? (1 = toe-in-the-wading-pool level of trust; 10 = high-dive level of trust)

1   2   3   4   5   6   7   8   9   10

TATTOO THIS ON YOUR BRAIN:

"Those who trust in the LORD will lack no good thing" (Psalm 34:10).

Think of three things you have trouble trusting God for. Write them on sticky notes, and every morning, thank him out loud that you can trust him to _____, _____, and _____.

OPEN COMMUNICATION

On a scale of 1 to 10, how open is your communication with God? (1 = like talking to Great-Aunt Mildred—awkward, brief, and only when I have to; 10 = like talking to my best friend—all the time, about everything)

1   2   3   4   5   6   7   8   9   10

TATTOO THIS ON YOUR BRAIN:

"Come close to God, and God will come close to you" (James 4:8).

DON'T FEEL ALONE if you have trouble talking to someone you can't see. We all feel that way sometimes. Try these exercises to help you: pray out loud; write down your prayers and pray them back to God; get down on your knees and talk to him; go outside to your favorite place and talk while you walk or look at beautiful scenery; think of 20 things you can thank God for.

At what times do you feel closest to God?

....

....

What tends to hold you back from intimacy with God?

....

....

TATTOO THIS ON YOUR BRAIN:

"Don't worry about anything; instead, pray about everything. Tell God what you need, and thank him for all he has done. Then you will experience God's peace, which exceeds anything we can understand. His peace will guard your hearts and minds as you live in Christ Jesus" (Philippians 4:6-7).

TAPE THE ABOVE VERSE AT YOUR COMPUTER, ON YOUR MIRROR, AND IN YOUR CAR.

Every time you start to worry about _____, say the verse out loud. Substitute the thing you're worried about: "Don't worry about _____; instead, pray about _____."

THE **PEOPLE** CONNECTION

THE LIE: I'll never be close to anyone.

THE TRUTH: God designed you to be close to other people.

THE BUZZ ON A BIBLE SHE

MARY OF BETHANY

STATUS:	Sister of Lazarus and Martha; lived in Bethany (two miles from Jerusalem). Jesus often did the bed-and-breakfast thing at their home.
HER CLAIM TO FAME:	Mary chose being with Jesus instead of doing other things. She was an intimacy receiver.
THE BACKDROP:	In Mary's day, women had low status and little respect. Tradition tells us that one of the prayers Jewish men prayed every morning was "Thank you, God, that you did not make me a slave, nor a heathen, nor a woman." But Jesus introduced a new respect for women, and Mary was one of the first in line to receive it.
SCENE ONE:	We meet Mary in her home when Jesus came to visit. While Martha was cooking, Mary sat at Jesus' feet and hung on his every word. When Martha complained that Mary wasn't helping in the kitchen, Jesus responded: "Martha, Martha, you are worried and troubled about many things. But one thing is needed, and Mary has chosen that good part, which will not be taken away from her" (Luke 10:41, NKJV).
SCENE TWO:	Mary shows up again after her brother, Lazarus, died. When Lazarus had gotten sick, Mary and Martha sent for Jesus, but he didn't show. By the time Jesus arrived, Lazarus was dead. Mary dropped down at Jesus' feet and poured out her heart: "Lord, if You had been here, my brother would not have died" (John 11:32, NKJV). Jesus wept with the sisters, and then he brought Lazarus back to life. Jesus' delay gave Mary and Martha the opportunity to know his character and power on a deeper level.
(FREEZE-FRAME:)	Before we move to our third encounter with Mary of Bethany, we can't help but wonder what happened between the verses of Scripture. Did Mary walk to the marketplace one day and overhear soldiers saying that they would crucify Jesus? Did she run back across the cobblestones to her home and touch the place where he always sat and she always listened? Did she glance at the bed where her now-alive brother slept? Did her heart ache at the possibility that her time with Jesus was coming to an end?
SCENE THREE:	Six days before Jesus' death, Jesus had dinner with his disciples at the home of one of his friends. As they reclined at the table, the door opened; enter Mary. A hush might have fallen over the room as she moved across the floor and bowed, once again, at Jesus' feet. She held a bottle of expensive perfume—perhaps the most valuable thing she owned. Performing the greatest act of honor a commoner could bestow on royalty, she poured it on his feet, despite objections that she was wasting it instead of selling it and giving the money to the poor. Jesus' defense was simple: "You will always have the poor among you, but you will not always have me" (John 12:8, NIV). And so the house was filled with the fragrance of perfume from someone who'd become an intimacy receiver at Jesus' feet.
WANT MORE DETAILS?	For the whole scoop, check out Luke 10:38-42; John 11:1-44; and John 12:1-11.

YOUR NEED FOR INTIMACY ISN'T YOUR IDEA.

God himself created you for people-intimacy—the ability to connect with others on a deep level. In the Bible he says, "It is not good for the man to be alone" (Genesis 2:18). And that means you.

But God is a jealous God. Not that he doesn't want us to have relationships with other people. But he knows that no one else is worthy of having first place in our life besides him—and no one else will fill the hole in us like he can. You can't replace intimacy with him with intimacy with someone else. So nothing we're about to say about people-intimacy works unless you first take care of your intimacy with God. *Never, never think you can replace God-intimacy with people-intimacy.* If you do, you'll never find safe intimacy with anyone.

FRIENDS · BOYFRIEND · MENTORS
ACQUAINTANCES
MYSELF
GOD
SIBLINGS
PARENTS

SHE GETS PERSONAL

Who has broken intimacy with you?

Who have you been able to connect with on an intimate level?

GiRL TALK!

With a friend, read these statements written by teens in our SHE survey. What should they watch out for? (If you get stuck, take a look at "Test Your Intimacy IQ" on page 40.)

? KATHERINE, 18: I've been together with my boyfriend for eight months. I tell him everything about my life, family, friends. I'm never stressed about our relationship or what he thinks of me. He helps me keep my head on straight.

? CHRISSY, 16: My boyfriend and I have been together for a long time, and the relationship is based on a need for each other and just wanting to be together.

? AMANDA, 15: My guy friend and I always have fun together no matter what we do. . . . We always find new things to do together so that we do not get bored. We are just happy when we get to spend time together. I trust him with any and all of my personal issues, secrets, problems, joys, frustrations. He listens to me when I talk and is always there to support me when I need it. I feel as if I can call him up in the middle of the night if I need to talk and he makes me feel good.

? TIFFANIE, 19: I love my job as a nanny. The mother has become more like a big sister and best friend to me than a boss. She's an authority figure but someone I also consider a mentor.

WHAT IS HONESTY?

Honesty: the freedom to be who you are, without pretending

Honesty: speaking from your heart and sharing your feelings and opinions

Honesty: being real with each other, whether you feel sad or happy, busy or bored

PEOPLE LIE FOR LOTS OF DIFFERENT REASONS: to protect themselves, to hide something, to try and get what they want, or because they believe their honesty might come back to haunt them. Some people think lying solves problems, but it usually creates more.

DO YOU BELIEVE ME?

Name someone under each of these categories and rank your honesty with them on a scale of 1–10 (10 being the highest).

Family

1　2　3　4　5　6　7　8　9　10

Friends

1　2　3　4　5　6　7　8　9　10

Boyfriend

1　2　3　4　5　6　7　8　9　10

Acquaintances

1　2　3　4　5　6　7　8　9　10

Under what circumstances do you find it most difficult to be honest?

What steps can you take to be more committed to honesty in your relationships?

WHAT IS TRUST?

Trust: the foundation of a healthy relationship

Trust: knowing that someone has your well-being in mind and will keep his or her promises to you

Trust: being yourself and working to bring out the best in the other person

DO YOU TRUST ME?

Only God is completely trustworthy. At some point, every person in your life will let you down (and you'll let other people down too). But that doesn't mean we should stop trusting. It means we have to forgive and choose to trust again anyway. How can you tell who is worthy of your trust?

Who in your life is trustworthy?

Who in your life is untrustworthy?

What can you do to make sure *you* are a trustworthy friend?

Name someone under each of these categories and rank your trust with them on a scale of 1–10 (10 being most trusted).

Family

1　2　3　4　5　6　7　8　9　10

Friends

1　2　3　4　5　6　7　8　9　10

Boyfriend

1　2　3　4　5　6　7　8　9　10

Acquaintances

1　2　3　4　5　6　7　8　9　10

WHAT IS OPEN COMMUNICATION?

Open communication: being able to talk freely and often and without judgment

Open communication: learning about each other on a deeper level

Open communication: statements like "I'm here for you," "Do you want to talk about it?" and "I understand"

ARE YOU THE REAL DEAL?

Name someone under each of these categories and rank your ability to communicate with that person on a scale of 1–10 (10 being most easy to communicate).

Family

1　2　3　4　5　6　7　8　9　10

Friends

1　2　3　4　5　6　7　8　9　10

Boyfriend

1　2　3　4　5　6　7　8　9　10

Acquaintances

1　2　3　4　5　6　7　8　9　10

LEVELS OF
COMMUNICATION

1 CHITCHAT
2 FACTS
3 IDEAS/JUDGMENTS
4 FEELINGS
5 OPEN/HONEST DISCUSSION

Identify the level of intimacy each of these interactions reflects:

" I don't like to be around him. I am hurt by the things he says. "

" I saw our history teacher at the mall. "

" Those shoes are awful! "

" I feel like I can talk to you about anything. "

" What's for lunch? "

(Answers: 4, 2, 3, 5, 1)

Identify someone in your life who fits into each of these levels of communication.

CHITCHAT:

....

FACTS:

....

IDEAS/JUDGMENTS:

....

FEELINGS:

....

OPEN/HONEST DISCUSSION:

....

SHEism: A truly intimate SHE is a girl who finds intimacy with God and then allows him to guide her toward finding safe intimacy with others.

SHE ASKS

JADA (17)

I have a guy friend who I've known for more than a year. We've just been best friends, and we can talk about everything. We know a lot about each other. Lately, though, we've been looking at each other in different ways, and our time together has gotten a little less comfortable. I think we might be becoming more than friends. If this is true, what is the healthy way to proceed? What should we do and not do?

REBECCA SAYS

It sounds like you and your guy friend have laid a healthy foundation for your potential relationship. Once you both know for sure that this is deeper than being "just friends," the next step is to talk openly and honestly about where you're at in your feelings for each another. Then commit to pray about what God would have you do. I believe that it is wise to begin dating/courting someone only when you are a couple of years away from the possibility of being married. The earlier you date, the more pressure you put on yourselves to go further physically.

GiRL TALK!

DO THEY HAVE WHAT IT TAKES?

Write down the qualities you're looking for in a friend and the qualities you are looking for in a boyfriend. You can write about personality traits, values, looks, or anything else. The more detailed you make it, the better.

Turn all of the negatives into positives. This encourages you to focus on what you want, not on what you don't want. For example, instead of saying, "I don't want a boyfriend who is possessive," you might say, "I want a boyfriend who trusts me."

Get specific. Review your list to see if any of your wants are vague. "A boyfriend who sticks up for people who are made fun of" is clearer than "a nice boyfriend."

Decide which of the characteristics on your list are musts, which are qualities you'd like, and which would be a nice extra. Put the corresponding symbol in the box beside each trait.

! must have
+ would like, but not essential
* nice bonus

QUALITIES I WANT IN A FRIEND

- ☐ _____
- ☐ _____
- ☐ _____
- ☐ _____
- ☐ _____
- ☐ _____

QUALITIES I WANT IN A BOYFRIEND

- ☐ _____
- ☐ _____
- ☐ _____
- ☐ _____
- ☐ _____
- ☐ _____

DO YOU HAVE WHAT IT TAKES?

Now make a list of what you have to offer in a relationship below. Be as honest as possible. Don't gloss over your true weaknesses, but don't be too hard on yourself either.

STRENGTHS I BRING TO A RELATIONSHIP

....
....

WEAKNESSES I BRING TO A RELATIONSHIP

....
....

THEY've Been There

If your parents get under your skin sometimes, you're not alone. Though you may hit some bumps in the road in your intimacy with your parents, your relationship doesn't have to continue to go downhill. Work really hard at your relationships with these people God gave you for all your life. They are the only parents you'll ever have. Here are some intimacy-enhancing suggestions for you to do with your parents:

- Take a walk and ask your parents about their friends when they were your age and what their relationship with their parents was like.

- Ask about a birthday or other special event they especially remember.

- Take a drive with your mom or dad.

- Tell them one thing you really appreciate about them. Then ask them what one way they would like for you to change. Hopefully they'll do the same for you.

- Talk about things that are going well in your relationship and ways you can improve your relationship now and in the days ahead.

SHE SPEAKS

MADELINE (16)

I would like to say my most intimate relationship is with God, but it's probably with my best friend—because we tell each other everything and because we know we can trust each other. And we always ask each other for advice on pretty much everything we think we need it on. So I think the fact that we can be so open with one another makes our relationship special, but it's not as special as it could be if I knew how to find intimacy with God. I wish someone would show me how.

SHE IS FEMININE

LIVE OUT WHAT IT MEANS TO BE A WOMAN IN THE SAFETY OF GOD'S WAY.

God created human beings in his own image. In the image of God he created them; male and female he created them.

Genesis 1:27

DO YOU HAVE WHAT IT TAKES TO BE A WOMAN?

It's a little confusing to even know what it means to be feminine when there are about a billion different versions of it thrown at you. Who decides the prerequisites to womanhood anyway? Is it "the Plastics"—the popular girls from the movie *Mean Girls*?

The Plastics' Girlworld Rules:

YOU MUST WEAR PINK ON WEDNESDAYS.

YOU CAN'T WEAR A TANK TOP TWO DAYS IN A ROW.

YOU CAN WEAR YOUR HAIR IN A PONYTAIL ONLY ONCE A WEEK.

YOU CAN WEAR JEANS OR TRACK PANTS ONLY ON FRIDAYS.

There has to be more to womanhood than that. Webster's dictionary tells us that femininity is "the quality or nature of the female sex." But what does that mean in real life?

Being feminine is more confusing now than ever before. And you are left to sort it out and decide who you are supposed to be in this role called woman you have been born into. So let's forget about the *Mean Girls* rules and talk about what it really means to be feminine—God's way.

Serve one another in love.
Galatians 5:13

FEMINISM POP QUIZ

1 How would you define a feminist woman?

a) A woman who makes sure females have the same opportunities as men

b) A powerful woman who steps on men and everyone else in her way to get what she wants

c) A woman with a political agenda to advance the pro-choice movement

d) A woman who empowers other women so they don't get trampled on

e) Other:_____

2 What is your emotional reaction to the term *feminism*? Circle how you feel:

positive	angry
negative	proud
secure	threatened
anxious	determined
supportive	empowered

3 Women should have political rights equal to those of men (the right to hold office, the right to vote, etc.).

Agree   Disagree   Undecided

4 Women should have the same economic rights as men (the right to hold the same jobs, the right to earn the same amount of money for the same job, the right to own property, etc.).

Agree   Disagree   Undecided

5 Women should have the same social rights as men (equal opportunities for relationships, respect, reputation, etc.).

Agree   Disagree   Undecided

6 In our society, women have the same political, economic, and social rights as men.

Agree   Disagree   Undecided

FEMININITY POP QUIZ

1 How would you define a feminine woman?

a) An old-fashioned woman who became extinct along with her record player

b) A woman who is weak and can't survive without a man

c) A woman who has learned to embrace her God-given identity as a female

d) A woman who is trying to balance her role in a world that expects her to be tough

e) Other:_____

2 Who or what has influenced your views on femininity?

3 Do you think femininity and masculinity share any traits?

HOW WE ENDED UP IN **FEMINIST-VILLE**

LET'S GO WAAAAAY BACK . . . to the last century, in fact. In the 1960s a woman named Betty Friedan published a book called *The Feminine Mystique*, which officially launched the feminist movement. She insisted that the women of her day felt unhappy and stifled with their lives as they asked themselves, *Is this all there is?*

Since then, women have gone out in search of finding it ALL—those pieces that seem to be missing to make our life totally complete. We have gained more rights, reputation, and respect than any generation before ever dreamed. But while some good things have come from the feminist movement, negative consequences have resulted too.

The new rights and privileges we've earned were added to the ones we already owned. What that means is someday—in addition to your roles as a wife, a mother, and a friend—you will also be expected to have a career, make a name for yourself, and establish your own independent reputation. We are able to participate in the same sports, earn the same college degrees, and work at the same jobs as men—but we're

still supposed to look gorgeous. We didn't subtract anything before we added all these new assignments. That translates to us—and specifically to you—as pressure, and lots of it.

You aspire to be a doctor someday, but today you worry about your weight. You play for the girls' basketball team, but you're afraid of getting attacked on the way to your car. You speak at a national youth convention, but you find it hard to convince your boyfriend you want to stay pure until marriage. You want to take advantage of every opportunity offered to you, but you can't possibly do it, so guilt and exhaustion diminish the rewards of the things you do accomplish. All this takes time. It takes work. And it takes a lot out of you.

SHE'S BEEN THERE

Do this exercise with a trusted, godly woman (such as your mom, your grandma, a family friend, or your youth pastor). Learn from her experiences about what it means to be feminine.

Lots of words are used to describe today's woman, from one extreme to another. Fill in the dot on the scale where you see yourself for each set of words. Then have your mentor do the same using a different color.

INDEPENDENT	O	O	O	O	O	O	O	O	DEPENDENT
RELIES ON HERSELF	O	O	O	O	O	O	O	O	RELIES ON OTHERS
AGGRESSIVE	O	O	O	O	O	O	O	O	SUBMISSIVE
ASSERTIVE	O	O	O	O	O	O	O	O	YIELDING
STOIC	O	O	O	O	O	O	O	O	EMOTIONAL
TAKES RISKS	O	O	O	O	O	O	O	O	FEARS CHANGE
COMPETITIVE	O	O	O	O	O	O	O	O	COOPERATIVE
LEADER	O	O	O	O	O	O	O	O	SUPPORTER
STRONG	O	O	O	O	O	O	O	O	GENTLE
DECISIVE	O	O	O	O	O	O	O	O	INDECISIVE
FORCEFUL	O	O	O	O	O	O	O	O	SOFT-SPOKEN
DOES HER OWN THING	O	O	O	O	O	O	O	O	GOES WITH THE CROWD
ANALYZER	O	O	O	O	O	O	O	O	FEELER

Which of these traits do you most want to develop in yourself?

1.

2.

3.

Which of these traits do you most want to change in yourself?

1.

2.

3.

REBECCA SAYS

One of the things that greatly concerns me about women's life decisions is the extremely strong focus on career. In generations past, women were respected for being wonderful wives and mothers. Now it seems that unless you go to college, get a degree, and go on to execute a full-fledged career, then you haven't really "made it" as a woman. Don't buy into our culture's way of thinking. If you feel called to go to college, go. If your dream is to be a wife and mother, then don't feel bad about learning the tricks of the trade at home!

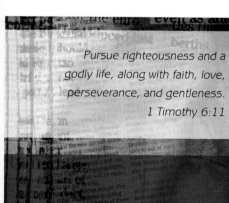

Pursue righteousness and a godly life, along with faith, love, perseverance, and gentleness.
1 Timothy 6:11

SHE SPEAKS

TAYLOR (17)
Summer jobs were few and far between in my town. I applied for one at the same time someone I knew did. Though we had the same qualifications, she got the job because she was louder, bolder, and tougher than I was. Whatever happened to being a lady?

SHE GETS PERSONAL

Think about a time when you felt you needed to be tougher after someone walked all over you or took advantage of you.

Think about a time when you were acting tough, but you ended up feeling less feminine.

Which side do you need to work on more: your tough side or your tender side?

What are some ways you can work on that side?

YEAH, BUT . . .

- If I'm tender, everybody will take advantage of me.
- If I'm tender, everybody will know who I really am.
- If I'm tough, everybody will think I'm masculine.
- If I'm tough, everybody will stay away from me.
- Other:_____

SO HOW DO WE FIND THE BALANCE BETWEEN TOUGH AND TENDER?
True femininity embraces both these qualities in a fairly equal way. We need to be *tough* enough to protect ourselves as well as our goals and dreams . . . but not so tough that we step on people along the way. We need to be *tender* enough to find intimacy with God and others . . . but not so tender that we are taken advantage of.

The Bible describes the perfect love of God the Father as including both tough and tender dimensions. Isaiah gives us a picture of a tough God:

> The Sovereign LORD is coming in power. He will rule with a powerful arm. See, he brings his reward with him as he comes. ISAIAH 40:10

But in the very next verse he shows us the tender side of God:

> He will feed his flock like a shepherd. He will carry the lambs in his arms, holding them close to his heart. He will gently lead the mother sheep with their young. ISAIAH 40:11

We find that same connection between toughness and tenderness in the New Testament. Jesus was tough when he needed to be—like when he saw the merchants treating the Temple with disrespect.

He knocked over the tables of the money changers and the chairs of those selling doves. He said to them, "The Scriptures declare, 'My Temple will be called a house of prayer,' but you have turned it into a den of thieves!" MATTHEW 21:12-13

But Jesus balanced that toughness with tenderness toward his followers.

> Take my yoke upon you. Let me teach you, because I am humble and gentle at heart, and you will find rest for your souls. MATTHEW 11:29

God wants us to strive for this balance too. According to God's standards, the beauty of the truly feminine woman is found in her "gentle and quiet spirit, which is so precious to God" (1 Peter 3:4).

FEMININITY (GOD'S WAY)
the gentle and quiet—
but spirited—woman.

Be strong in the Lord and in his mighty power. Ephesians 6:10

PAGE 57

SHE ASKS

KELSEY (15)

I come from a single-parent home where money is tight, and I have a lot of responsibilities. I've been let down a lot by people. My dad doesn't come through with money to support us or time to be with us when he says he will. So I feel like I've hardened. I try to make people think I don't need other people since I don't trust them anyway. Because of this, people stay away, and I don't have a best friend. Why can't people see that I really need them—I'm just afraid to say so?

REBECCA SAYS

Years ago, I was devastated when a friend repeatedly lied to me and made me doubt everything else he had ever said. I let myself trust him but ended up feeling betrayed. One evening I sat on my parents' bed, crying to my mum. I recall saying that I didn't want to become hard, bitter, and shut off to this person. But as I said to her that night, "It hurts so bad to stay soft."

Pain threatens our femininity because the feminine woman has a side that is tender, open, and wisely trusting. In any painful situation, we have one of two choices: We can become overly tough and shut off to the point that we don't feel our pain and we allow bitterness to breed. Or we can stay open, grieve our hurt, and keep our tender side tender. We need to have a balance of these two things: softness and strength.

GIRL TALK!

✳ List every activity you're involved in right now:

. . . .

. . . .

. . . .

✳ Think back over the last week. Fill in the things that took up your time in the chart below.

	MORNING	AFTERNOON	EVENING
MONDAY			
TUESDAY			
WEDNESDAY			
THURSDAY			
FRIDAY			
SATURDAY			
SUNDAY			

✳ What emotions did you feel while keeping up with the schedule above? Here's a sample list to get you thinking:

embarrassed	bored
proud	excited
overwhelmed	exhausted
fulfilled	energized

✳ Describe the three greatest pressures you feel in your life today:

1 . . . .

2 . . . .

3 . . . .

✳ Is there anything you need to change about your current schedule?

. . . .

. . . .

. . . .

Always be humble and gentle. Be patient with each other, making allowance for each other's faults because of your love.
Ephesians 4:2

She is clothed with strength and dignity, and she
laughs without fear of the future.
Proverbs 31:25

THE TENDER YOU

THE LIE: If I'm a gentle and quiet woman, I'll get stepped on by others and never achieve anything worthwhile.

THE TRUTH: YOU CAN BE TENDER AND STILL NOT ALLOW YOURSELF TO BE TAKEN ADVANTAGE OF OR OVERLOOKED.

A gentle and quiet spirit . . .
is so precious to God.
1 Peter 3:4

TOUGH STUFF QUIZ

What would you do in each of the following situations? (Be honest!)

1 Your mother wants you to wear a sweater to school because she thinks it's cold. You aren't cold at all.
a) You roll your eyes and say, "Give me a break! I'm sick of you always wanting me to wear a sweater."
b) You say nothing and wear the sweater.
c) You say, "Mom, I'm not cold, so I don't plan to wear a sweater today."

2 Your best friend wants to borrow your new outfit. You haven't even worn it yet, and you really don't want to lend it to her.
a) You say, "Why don't you get your own outfit! There's no way I'm going to give you mine!"
b) You lie and tell her it's in the wash.
c) You say, "I don't want to lend you my new outfit. Let's go through your closet and see what we can find."

3 Your father wants you to help him wash the car, but you have an important test tomorrow.
a) You say, "Dad, I'm not your slave. Don't you know I have work to do?"
b) You ask your mom to tell him you can't help.
c) You say, "Dad, I'd like to help, but I have too much studying to do tonight. Give me a little more notice, and I'll make time to help."

4 The most popular girl in class wants to copy your homework because she didn't have time to finish hers.
a) You say, "Don't you know that's cheating? I'm sorry, but you'll have to get it done on time next time."
b) You let her copy the paper.
c) You say, "You know, I'm not comfortable letting people copy my homework. But we have a few minutes before class—let me help you get started."

5 Your teacher asks you to stay and help tutor another student after class, but you have arranged an outing with your best friend.
a) You say, "I have better things to do. No way!"
b) You stay after school and cancel your plans.
c) You say, "I'd like to help, but I have other plans today. I'm free tomorrow, or maybe one of the other students in our class could help."

· ·

TOTAL UP THE NUMBER OF A'S, B'S, AND C'S YOU HAD.

MOSTLY A'S: You may be too tough. You do a good job setting boundaries for yourself, but you are in danger of drowning out the tender side of you. TIP: Before each thing you say today, think about your tone. Is it gentle and loving? If not, do some quick mental tune-ups before you open your mouth!

MOSTLY B'S: You may be too tender. It's obvious you care about other people and their feelings, but you're in danger of ignoring the tough side of you. TIP: Before you go along with someone else's plans, think about how this decision will affect you. Do you need to stand up for yourself?

MOSTLY C'S: You are learning a good balance between being tough and being tender. Keep up the good work as you continue to live out God's definition of femininity. It's a lifelong process!

She is energetic and strong, a hard worker.
Proverbs 31:17

REBECCA SAYS

When I began in music, my dad, who is my manager, encouraged me in my concerts to share a few words before one of my songs. He stressed the importance of connecting in this way with the audience. On my first tour, when I was 13, I memorized every line of my "speech." At the time, I objected to having to do something that didn't come naturally. I could sing all day long on stage, but I had no confidence in my ability to speak before a crowd. But as I prayed to be used by God and practiced what I knew to be something I was called to do, my sharing grew to be natural and powerful, despite my lack of self-confidence. Today some people tell me that my words from the stage have had more impact on them than my music. Being pushed to share at such an early age helped to "toughen my skin." We all need to find a balance between the toughness and tenderness God has created within us.

THE TOUGH YOU

THE LIE: If I'm a spirited woman, I'll get hardened.

YOU CAN BE SPIRITED AND STILL BE FEMININE.

GIRL TALK!

Along with a friend or two, describe ways you can be tough but tender in the examples below:

1 Your friend was at a party that got busted for underage drinking.

2 You're interviewing for a summer job as a waitress, and you want to show godly femininity.

3 You're facing someone who is bullying you at school.

4 Your best friend makes plans to go to the movies with you, then asks if she can bring along someone you really don't want to spend time with.

5 Your father's golfing buddy is coming to dinner, along with his young son, who you watched last time. The child was a terror, and you don't want to babysit.

6 The most popular girl in your class is in charge of the school booth at the carnival. She asks you to be on the cleanup committee, but you'd rather be on the decoration committee and you know there's still room.

7 Your teacher gives you a C on a paper you feel you deserve at least a B on.

SHE ASKS

ALEXIS (14)

I'm not as frilly as other girls in my class. I'd rather do sports and hang around with my guy friends. Someone called me a lesbian the other day. It really hurt. What can I do to keep this from happening and at the same time still be who I am?

REBECCA SAYS

I grew up hangin' with the boys too. Hey, I lived in a house with five brothers—I couldn't be more comfortable with guys. I have always been a bit of a tomboy . . . more into LEGOs than Barbies. I don't think your femininity depends on your frilliness. I think there is something very feminine about a girl who feels comfortable in her own skin, who warmly embraces others, who feels safe and protected, and who exudes a softness because of her closeness to Jesus. This is the opposite of the overly independent, shut-off, hardened women our culture seems to want us to be.

Be strong and courageous!
Do not be afraid or discouraged.
For the LORD your God is with you
wherever you go.
Joshua 1:9

THE BUZZ ON A BIBLE SHE

DEBORAH

FEMININE FACTOR: Deborah lived in a man's world that looked down on women. Women could not vote or hold office; they also couldn't own property, make business deals, or enter certain parts of the Temple. But despite these strikes against her, Deborah discovered true femininity by following God's rules.

STATUS: Deborah was a wife, but she also worked outside the home as a judge—the only woman of twelve judges who ruled during that era of Israel's history. Many of the rulers before Deborah had been ungodly men, and Israel had suffered because of it. But Deborah made up her mind early that she would rule according to God's rules.

HER RÉSUMÉ: She settled disputes for people from all over Israel.
She gave God-given prophesies about the future of her country.
She gave advice to the top army generals.
She marched to battle with all the tough guys.
She was a singer and a songwriter.

THE TOUGH DEBORAH: Deborah's toughness kept her protected and helped her hold her own in a man's world. She didn't step on others to get where she was. She merely lived up to her responsibilities, which had been given to her by God. Because her confidence was not based on natural strengths, natural things like wars and other people did not intimidate her. Neither did the men who surrounded her. She gave up her right to be in charge and acknowledged that the only rights she had were the ones God gave her.

THE TENDER DEBORAH: Her tenderness prevented her from trying to be a lone ranger, and she encouraged other people to fulfill their roles too. Deborah understood the delicate balance between leading and submitting. She worked as a team with others, both at home and on the job. At the same time, she brought out the best in others by helping them to excel rather than forcing them to compete.

HER SECRET: She was able to have courage going into battle because she knew the Lord marched ahead of her (Judges 4:14). As we fight our own battles for godly femininity, we can have that same assurance.

WANT MORE DETAILS? For the whole scoop, check out Judges 4–5.

SHEism: A truly feminine **SHE** is someone wh
In the process **SHE** becomes a gentl

balances her tough and tender sides.
and quiet—but spirited—girl of God.

SHE ASKS

HEATHER (19)

What does it mean to be feminine in a dating relationship? I like to be treated respectfully by the guy, but I was brought up to be able to take care of myself.

REBECCA SAYS

I have learned a lot about being a gentle and quiet woman through God's rules about submission, but like you, I still struggle at times in this area. Once while on my Romanian mission trip, I had been asked to carry a brand-new window from the car into the girls' home where I was working. One of the girls who lived there, a former street kid, had broken the window, and this was the replacement.

Catalin, the man in charge of the home, asked me to put it on the floor in the stairwell landing. This didn't make sense to my practical woman mind. The floor was tiled. If the window fell over, it would be history. In addition, kids were constantly flying down the stairwell, so there was a good chance it could get broken. I pointed this out to Catalin and asked if he'd prefer that I put it in a carpeted room instead. He said no, that it would be fine in the stairwell. I kept my mouth shut and then turned and carried the window . . . into the carpeted room!

When Catalin found out what I had done, he made a tongue-in-cheek comment that marriage (and submission) might one day be a bit of an adjustment for me. Though Catalin's comment was a friendly jab, the truth of it stuck with me. I should've recognized that it was his window and his home, and I should have respected his authority to have the last word—even when I thought my way was best.

Submission means that we voluntarily acknowledge the leadership responsibilities of others. It doesn't mean we disrespect ourselves or consider ourselves less valuable than someone else, whether that person is a friend, a boyfriend, a parent, a teacher, or a youth leader. God's direction for you is that you step aside and allow him to work through the gifts he's given them. God's plan for them is that they not abuse that trust or submission. If someone is trying to make you do something that is ungodly, then you must say no. God is your ultimate authority.

SHE IS BEAUTIFUL

FOLLOW THESE HEALTH AND BEAUTY
SECRETS THAT WON'T WRINKLE
OR GO OUT OF STYLE!

The God who slung the stars across the heavens
. . . that God, the King, has always been taken
with you. You have been noticed. He thinks
you're beautiful, the glass slipper fits, the music is
playing, and He's asking you to dance.
ANGELA THOMAS, *Do You Think I'm Beautiful?*

God has made everything beautiful for its own time.
Ecclesiastes 3:11

YOUR REMOTE CONTROL COULD TELL YOU THAT WE'RE PRETTY MUCH ADDICTED TO BEAUTY.

One of MTV's latest reality shows, *I Want a Famous Face*, takes us on the journeys of people who have gone through painful and sometimes dangerous reconstructive surgery—all to look like their favorite celebrity. We're not talking makeovers here—we're talking plastic surgery, bone restructuring . . . even transgender operations. Here are some of the reasons the participants want a famous face:

• "Mia believes she already naturally looks like Britney [Spears], she just needs the breasts. She hopes that with her breast implants, she will be able to quit her day job and make it big-time as an entertainer."

• "I knew that if I imitated Brad Pitt's appearance . . . I would be happy with mine," Mike says.

• Sha says she chose to look like Pamela Anderson "because I think she is a beautiful woman, who is smart in her business, and knows how to take advantage of every opportunity that comes with being beautiful and has turned it into a great career, which is something that I hope to do."[1]

Don't be concerned about the outward beauty of fancy hairstyles, expensive jewelry, or beautiful clothes. You should clothe yourselves instead with the beauty that comes from within, the unfading beauty of a gentle and quiet spirit, which is so precious to God.
1 Peter 3:3-4

SHE SPEAKS

JENNA (15)

Girls are pressured into being skinny. If you are overweight, you won't be popular. Sometimes you can't get a guy. People don't get to know you for your personality because they can't get past the fact that you are not skinny. So a lot of girls go out of their way to be skinny so they will be liked by their peers. I'm skinny, but I find myself wishing that I was skinnier a lot because I see some girls who are perfect.

SHE SPEAKS

LEIGH (19)

I grew up in a Christian home. My father was a pastor. I was a cheerleader in middle school, high school, and college, so beauty always mattered. I was insecure about it, however. I would see friends accepted by boys more than I was while I secretly felt I was prettier, though the boys didn't seem to agree. So the struggles and compromise began. I didn't concentrate on how beautiful I was to God. I allowed the standards for my beauty to be set by other people. In my college cheerleading outfits, I saw myself becoming a temptation to men and felt uncomfortable in them. But I kept thinking, *I'm an adult in college now. My parents aren't here.* I wanted acceptance, and I compromised my image, including my dress, so I could be beautiful to others. Because I was a cheerleader and people recognized me on campus, I felt I had to be beautiful all the time. And though I had every reason to feel secure, I wondered if I was pretty to anyone other than my boyfriend. So I lost my purity to him, and we continued in a sexual relationship for many months.

SHE SPEAKS

SHELBY (13)

Teens are pressured by magazines and TV to dress, talk, and act like the girls shown in them. Society wants us to be exactly like the models in magazines and television, which creates very high standards for us to follow. Nobody can be exactly like them, but we keep trying. The pressures have caused us to do things we wished we hadn't, and it has even pushed people to kill themselves because they couldn't fit in and be like everyone else.

ince you were a little girl, the quest to be beautiful has bombarded you at every turn. From children's stories such as "Sleeping Beauty" and "The Ugly Duckling" that you read to the Barbie dolls that you played with to the comments such as "She's darling" or "What a pretty little girl you are" that you heard—face it, beauty has become an all-consuming priority!

Now that you are a teen, you are under even more pressure to be beautiful. TV, movies, and music tell you that if you want to be beautiful you have to look a certain way, dress a certain way, and have a certain type of body.

FAQs FREQUENTLY ASKED QUESTIONS

WHAT IS ANOREXIA?

Anorexia: I refuse to keep a healthy body weight.

Anorexia: I have a distorted view of what I look like.

Anorexia: I have an abnormal fear of getting fat.

WHAT IS BULIMIA?

Bulimia: I cycle between binging (overeating) and purging (self-induced vomiting or the use of laxatives to rid the body of food).

WHAT IS COMPULSIVE OVEREATING?

Compulsive overeating: I binge (overeat) when I'm not hungry.

Compulsive overeating: I continue to eat without thinking about the consequences.

DID YA KNOW . . .

About 10 million Americans suffer from eating disorders, and 90 percent of those afflicted are age 20 or under.

One out of every 100 young women between 10 and 20 is starving herself.

Four percent of college-age women have bulimia.

Anorexia and bulimia affect primarily people in their teens and twenties, but studies report both disorders in children as young as 6 and individuals as old as 76.

Sixty percent of adult Americans, both male and female, are overweight. About 34 percent are obese, meaning they are 20 percent or more above normal, healthy weight, mostly as a result of a binge eating disorder.

Without treatment, up to 20 percent of people with serious eating disorders die. With treatment, that number falls to 2 to 3 percent.

With treatment, about 60 percent of people with eating disorders recover. Despite treatment, about 20 percent of people with eating disorders make only partial recoveries.[2]

SHE SPEAKS

ELIZABETH (17)

My dad jokes around all the time. He would say, "There you are eating again." I think a father's love is just so important in a girl's life. I never felt like I had his love because he never really said it. He's not around a whole lot. It's not that great a relationship.

I wouldn't say I was anorexic. I was bulimic for a little while. I felt like I was fat from my dad telling me that. I take to heart what he says because of who he is and what he says. I don't have self-esteem or self-respect because it was never really laid into me that I am special—a princess.

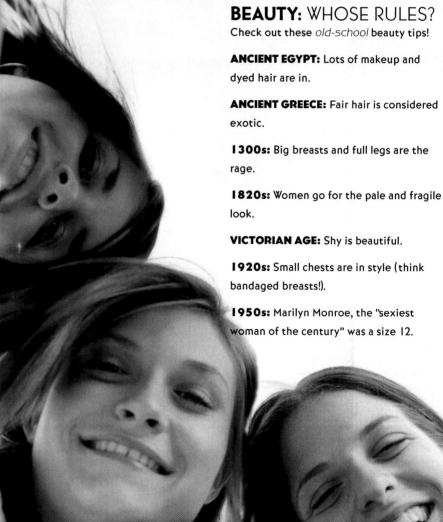

BEAUTY: WHOSE RULES?

Check out these *old-school* beauty tips!

ANCIENT EGYPT: Lots of makeup and dyed hair are in.

ANCIENT GREECE: Fair hair is considered exotic.

1300s: Big breasts and full legs are the rage.

1820s: Women go for the pale and fragile look.

VICTORIAN AGE: Shy is beautiful.

1920s: Small chests are in style (think bandaged breasts!).

1950s: Marilyn Monroe, the "sexiest woman of the century" was a size 12.

Is your eating disorder your best friend?

You are not alone.

There is hope.

" I could go on and on about how Remuda Ranch changed my life. Thank you so much."

R E M U D A
Nourishment for Life *Ranch*
Programs for Anorexia and Bulimia
RemudaRanch.com

800-445-1900

Eating Disorders

Unplanned Pregnancy

Depression

Sexual Abuse

Addictions...

There is hope...

"Mercy Ministries - A wonderful place where unconditional love conquers all and dreams of a magnificent future are restored."

www.mercyministries.com

mailing address: p.o. box 111060, nashville, tn 37222-1060   phone: 615-831-6987

"For I know the plans I have for you," declares the Lord, "plans to prosper you and not to harm you, plans to give you a hope and a future."

Jeremiah 29:11

REBECCA SAYS

I have played the comparison game too. This is an embarrassing confession, but once I recall tearing out a magazine ad that pictured a girl standing beside a car. She looked like what I thought I wanted to look like. She had toned arms, a slim figure, and beautiful, full hair. I kept this picture with me to supposedly help me achieve my goal. But I realized pretty quickly that this was only negative, that it was making me feel even more discontented with the unique way God created me. Basically, I was coveting what someone else had—which amounts to breaking one of the Ten Commandments. The other problem with comparing ourselves to other people—especially people in magazines—is that often these images aren't even realistic. With today's technology, most pictures are doctored to erase flaws or even shave off inches. And most models weigh less than what is considered healthy for their height.

GET REAL!

If store mannequins were real, they would be too thin to menstruate.

Of the 3 billion women in the world, only eight are supermodels.

The average American woman is 5'4" and weighs 144 pounds. The average model is 5'11" and weighs 117 pounds.

If Barbie were a real woman, she would be 6'0" and weigh 101 pounds. She would have a 39" bust, 19" waist, and 33" hips. Barbie wouldn't be able to walk because her lower body could not support her upper body.[3]

The LORD doesn't see things the way you see them. People judge by outward appearance, but the LORD looks at the heart.
1 Samuel 16:7

BEAUTY JAIL

We've all looked in the mirror only to see a face that didn't measure up to the current standards of beauty, and we've ended up feeling discouraged.

CAN YOU THINK OF ANYTHING OR ANY *THINGS* TO FILL IN THIS BLANK?

"I hate my _____!"

Sometimes you need to take a closer look to see just how extreme your discontent and dislike of your physical body has become.

BEAUTY QUIZ

Answer each of these questions honestly and give yourself the matching number of points.

1. I've dieted to lose weight during the last
   - 24 hours = 10 points
   - month = 5 points
   - year = 1 point
   - decade = 0 points

2. I look at other women's appearances and compare myself to them
   - almost always = 10 points
   - frequently = 5 points
   - rarely = 1 point
   - never = 0 points

3. I normally weigh myself
   - more than once a day = 10 points
   - daily = 5 points
   - monthly = 1 point
   - annually or at medical checkups = 0 points

4. When I am in public without makeup, I feel
   - ugly = 10 points
   - naked = 5 points
   - plain = 1 point
   - no different = 0 points

5. I worry about my weight and/or my appearance
   - once an hour or more = 10 points
   - off and on throughout the day = 5 points
   - a few times a week = 1 point
   - hardly ever = 0 points

6. Almost every time I eat, at least once I think about
   - how much I should weigh or how fat I am = 10 points
   - the number of calories I'm consuming = 5 points
   - ways to satisfy my hunger appropriately = 1 point
   - enjoying and being thankful for my meal = 0

7. When I look in the mirror, I usually see
   - every imperfection = 10 points
   - several imperfections = 5 points
   - a few imperfections = 1 point
   - me = 0 points

51-70 points = Trapped in beauty-myth jail

21–50 points = Handcuffed to the beauty myth

6–20 points = Have beauty myths under house arrest

0–5 points = Free!

SHE GETS PERSONAL

Yesterday, approximately how many minutes did you spend on your appearance (outer beauty)?

Yesterday, approximately how many minutes did you spend on your relationship with God and with other people (inner beauty)?

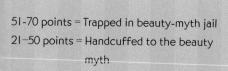

GOD'S **TEMPLE**

The problem with trying to measure up to the images we see on TV and in movies is that often girls do harmful things to their body. Too many young women are starving themselves or making themselves throw up to try to achieve the look they want. Others cut themselves to get attention, express hurt, or just to feel something. If you or someone you know is dealing with any of these issues, remember that if you are a Christian, your body belongs to God—it is not your own (see 1 Corinthians 6:19-20). When you hurt yourself, you hurt him too. During those times when you're feeling particularly low about your self-image, remind yourself that you should be focusing on your God-worth, not your self-worth. YOU ARE HIS TREASURE, HIS PRINCESS.

BEAUTY BY THE BOOK

THE BIBLE WAS WAY AHEAD OF US in exposing the beauty myth for what it is. It points out the *vanity*, *danger*, and *temporary* quality of mere personal attractions and instead calls attention to the higher and more permanent beauties of *mind*, *character*, and *personality*.

It's called outward versus inward beauty. The Book puts it this way:

> Don't be concerned about the outward beauty
> of fancy hairstyles, expensive jewelry, or beautiful clothes.
> You should clothe yourselves instead
> with the beauty that comes from within.
>
> 1 PETER 3:3-4

YEAH, BUT . . .

- I won't be accepted for who I am.

- I will still be compared to others and not measure up.

- People judge me by how I look before they get to know me.

- Other: _____

We know you've heard this talk about the inside package versus the outside package before. But our guess is that none of it has yet to change your beauty response. And we know you're probably thinking, *Inside beauty? Try telling that to the guys. They avoid describing us on the outside by saying we've "got a great personality" or we're "really nice."*

THE BIBLE IS NOT SAYING THAT THE OUTER APPEARANCE DOESN'T MATTER. IT'S SAYING: DON'T BE CONCERNED ABOUT THE OUTER BEAUTY.

Don't let it define you. Don't let it cause you undue stress. Don't make it your most important priority. Don't let it replace the more important parts of your life.

Outer beauty is nothing more than packaging. And unless the inner content is good, too, the outer display won't make any lasting difference.

DO **BE KNOWN** FOR THE INNER BEAUTY.

Outer beauty is the first impression someone gets of you; inner beauty is the second and lasting impression. We call it holistic beauty, and it's real, honest, and lasting. It reveals the contents on the inside of the package that enhance the outer. You can't fake holistic beauty—it's the way women look, feel, think, and act. It's the whole beauty shebang!

REBECCA SAYS

I once read this article in an Australian devotional, which says a lot about real beauty:

A beauty product company once asked people in a large city to send pictures, along with brief letters, describing the most beautiful woman they knew. Within weeks, thousands of letters came in.

One letter caught the attention of the employees and was soon passed on to the company president. It was written by a boy from a broken home, who lived in a run-down neighborhood. With lots of spelling corrections, an excerpt from his letter read: "A beautiful woman lives down the street from me. I visit her every day. She makes me feel like the most important kid in the world. We play checkers and she listens to my problems. She understands me. When I leave she always yells out the door that she's proud of me." The boy ended his letter saying, "This picture shows you that she is the most beautiful woman in the world, and one day I hope I have a wife as pretty as her."

Intrigued by the letter, the president asked to see the woman's picture. His secretary handed him the photograph of a smiling, toothless woman, well advanced in years, sitting in a wheelchair. Sparse gray hair was pulled back in a bun. The wrinkles that formed deep furrows on her face were somehow diminished by the twinkle in her eyes.

"We can't use this woman," exclaimed this president, smiling. "She would show the world that our products aren't necessary to be beautiful."[6]

COURTNEY (20)

I was never the cookie-cutter image of a beautiful child. Everyone used to say Ashley, my sister, was beautiful; Clint, my brother, was cute; and I was a good eater! My amazing appetite fueled my body to grow to six feet tall by the time I was 12. Yes, in sixth grade I was six feet tall! I looked down on most every guy, and I was a head above most girls. Most of my school years I felt awkward about my appearance and wanted so badly to look like everyone else. I wanted to be cute and petite and be able to find pants that were long enough for me—a 36 inseam in a size 2. But thanks to my involvement in sports, I appreciated my height for the advantages it gave me in other areas of my life.

As I got older, people started telling me that I should model and that I was stunning. While these compliments filled a void in my life, they were inconsistent with what I heard from my peers. Though people outside of school would compliment me, boys in school never asked me out. When a guy would ask me for my phone number at the mall, I would brag to my guy friends at school. I thought that maybe if they knew somebody else thought I was pretty, they would think so too. Why was it that grown-ups told me how lucky I was, yet I couldn't get a date to the dance? Toward the end of high school, guys started asking me out. It was then I started to realize that what they were attracted to was that I *wasn't* "normal." That I *did* stand out. That I *wasn't* a cookie cutter—I was me. And that I was more than enough.

What I wanted so badly in school would be the last thing that I want today. God used those awkward years of my life to create self-esteem that came from more than just my appearance. I learned how to get people to like me based on more than my looks. Today I am confident in my appearance and in many other things that "normally pretty" girls in school are struggling with. I once thought standing out was the biggest curse, but God is revealing to me that it is one of my greatest blessings!

SHE ASKS

MEAGEN (14)

Do you feel a lot of pressure to be skinny since you are always in the spotlight?

REBECCA SAYS

I have definitely struggled with my self-image. Being involved in the entertainment business, where image counts way too much, has only made matters worse. I've never been fine-featured or petite. My mom has always said I have "heavy bones." As I grew older, I felt this more keenly whenever I'd perform. I felt all the TV-induced insecurities that almost every other girl feels. Compared to the glamorous women I saw in the media, I was too shapely, too healthy looking. I truly believe that if it weren't for God's protection and my family's accountability, I could have started down an extremely dangerous path of trying to lose weight. I've got to be reminded constantly of the importance of internal beauty—a beauty that won't fade as I get older. "People judge by outward appearance, but the LORD looks at the heart" (1 Samuel 16:7). What matters is that I spend time with God so that he can beautify me—from the inside out.

THE LIE: IF I'M NOT SUPERMODEL BEAUTIFUL, THEN I DON'T MEASURE UP—I AM NOT ENOUGH.

THE TRUTH: YOU ARE FEARFULLY AND WONDERFULLY MADE.

You made all the delicate, inner parts of my body and knit me together in my mother's womb. Thank you for making me so wonderfully complex! Your workmanship is marvelous— how well I know it.
Psalm 139:13-14

THE BUZZ ON A BIBLE SHE

BATHSHEBA

BEAUTY FACTOR:	10
STATUS:	Married to Uriah, an honored and celebrated hero in the king's army
WRONG PLACE, WRONG TIME:	Spotted by King David while bathing on a rooftop
THE BIG OOPS:	Bathsheba was summoned to the palace of King David while her husband was at battle. They slept together, and she got pregnant. A panicky, wanting-to-cover-his-tracks David sent her husband to the front lines of battle. David gave the command. Uriah died.
WHAT WAS SHE THINKING?	Did she purposely place herself within David's view? Did she use her looks to get the guy? Did she flaunt her beauty? We're not sure, but we do know she didn't guard her heart or obey God's standards out of an inner, godly beauty.
HER PAY-UP:	A chain reaction of sorrow and curses on her family, including the death of her and David's baby boy and later the death of three of David's other sons.
BED, BATHSHEBA, & BEYOND:	It seems that somewhere along the line, Bathsheba repented. And somewhere along the line, God accepted her repentance, exchanged her sin for his grace, and then turned that sin into something he could use for his glory.
HER NEW REP:	Check out Proverbs 31:10-31. How does Scripture describe this wonder woman? She is virtuous, trustworthy, industrious, generous, strong, joyful, wise, kind, and God-fearing. As a result, her husband trusts her, she enriches his life, and she's worth more than "precious rubies." So who is this woman? Scripture tells us that King Lemuel wrote this chapter based on what his mother taught him. Many Bible scholars have said that King Lemuel was Solomon. And Solomon's mother was none other than Bathsheba—the woman whose inner beauty needed to develop so it was strong enough to guide and enhance her outer beauty.
WANT MORE DETAILS?	For the whole scoop, check out 2 Samuel 11-12.

DEAL.

Some of the things about both our outer and inner beauty cannot be changed. We just have to accept them as they are—end of story. Those qualities in our outer beauty include our hair and eye color and our skin tone. Unchangeable characteristics in our inner beauty include the ways we're gifted and the personality types we're born with.

Life, however, can be a continual journey of improvements, both externally and internally. We just need to make sure we keep our priorities in line.

WHAT YOUR MAKEUP IS SAYING ABOUT YOU BEHIND YOUR BACK

At first glance, another person learns a lot about you by observing your body language, hair, posture, dress, makeup, facial expressions, and movement of head and hair. We often don't realize how much power is in our look. It's screaming, though silent. That visual language counts for 60 to 65 percent of communication—more than the spoken message.

THE MIRROR QUIZ

Stand in front of a mirror. Close your eyes, then open them again. Objectively look at your makeup.

1. What does it say about you?

2. What adjectives would you use to describe your method of applying makeup?

3. Does your makeup say something different than you'd like?

4. How would you like someone to describe you after examining your makeup?

I want women to be modest in their appearance. They should wear decent and appropriate clothing and not draw attention to themselves by the way they fix their hair or by wearing gold or pearls or expensive clothes.

I Timothy 2:9

THE MIRROR-IMAGE QUIZ

You're going to need to stand in front of two mirrors for this one: a physical mirror and a soul mirror. Each question has two parts: what your outward appearance says about who you are, and what your words and actions communicate about you.

SEDUCTIVE?

Do you go for bright, wet lips, lots of mascara and eyeliner, and bright eye shadow?

Do your clothes reveal more than they should? Do you lead guys on with your flirting?

POWERFUL?

Are you hiding behind a mask: heavy eye makeup, angular blush movement, lots of foundation, and overemphasized brows?

Do you step on people who get in the way of your goals?

DARK?

Do you go for the pale-face-and-dark-eyes look?

Do you listen to depressing music and talk about dark stuff?

ATTENTION-SEEKING?

Do you choose quirky or rebellious clothes and makeup so you'll stand out?

Do you make loud comments in class or pull crazy stunts so people will notice you?

UNFEMININE?

Do you avoid makeup and flattering clothes to escape the way God created you as a woman?

Do you stuff down your sensitive side and put up a tough-girl image? Do you refuse to let your family and friends see your emotions?

LAZY?

Are your clothes and hair slobbish and disheveled, as if you don't think you're worth bothering with?

Do you choose couch-potato mode instead of building relationships, helping your parents, or spending time with God?

Thanks to Sue Cary Mayer, who has worked as a makeup artist for sitcom actors and actresses and other celebrities, for providing the inspiration for "The Mirror-Image Quiz."

YOU ARE BEAUTIFUL.

You grew up and became a beautiful jewel.

(Ezekiel 16:7)

YOU ARE TREASURED.

The LORD your God has chosen you to be his own special treasure.

(Deuteronomy 7:6)

YOU ARE
PRECIOUS.

The LORD's loved ones are precious to him.

(Psalm 116:15)

over your shoulder. Here's what *he* has to say about you:

YOU ARE HONORED.

You are precious to me. You are honored, and I love you.
(Isaiah 43:4)

YOU ARE ONE OF A KIND.

I knew you before I formed you in your mother's womb. Before you were born I set you apart.
(Jeremiah 1:5)

YOU ARE LOVED.

For he loves us with unfailing love.
(Psalm 117:2)

The more we live our life out before God,
the more beautiful we become.
Sue Cary Mayer, makeup artist

THE SHE IN THE MIRROR

1. Face yourself. From a seated or standing position, bend over from the waist and touch your knees, calves, or toes.

2. Now just hang there for a moment and let the blood rush to your face. Swing your body up and look at your refreshed image in the mirror.

3. Brush your hair back so you can see yourself fully. Look at your face.

4. Focus on each part: hairline, forehead, brows, temples, eyes, eyelashes, nose, cheekbones, cheeks, lips, teeth, jawline, chin, complexion. Don't dwell on anything that you have considered to be a negative in the past. Instead look at the unique quality of each of your features.

5. Next, concentrate on your entire face—the whole picture, the sum of those parts.

6. Now write a list of at least five of the positive aspects of your face. If you can easily come up with five, try 10. If you can't come up with any, you're thinking too negatively. Ask a friend for help. She will see them immediately.

....

....

....

....

....

....

....

SHE SPEAKS

MONET (17)
Last summer, I had the amazing opportunity to spend four weeks of my life in Botswana, Africa. There, with 90 other teenagers, I encountered and experienced God in more ways than I could have ever imagined. We had no bathrooms and we had no showers. The food was edible at best, and a violent stomach virus nearly crippled our team for a period of days. Our hair was matted with dirt, our hands were cracked and dry, and our feet were bruised and dirty. Yet never before did our hearts and bodies feel so beautiful. Never before did our inward character radiate so magnificently to the outside world. Never before had we felt God's pleasure bestowed so graciously on our lives. And for the first time we understood what Paul had meant in Romans 10:15 when he said, "How beautiful are the feet of messengers who bring good news!"

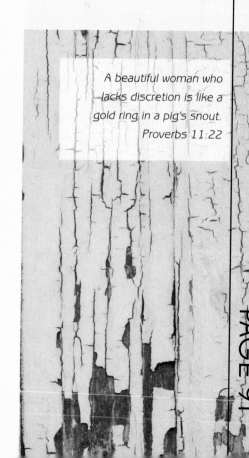

A beautiful woman who lacks discretion is like a gold ring in a pig's snout.
Proverbs 11:22

SO . . .
WHATCHA GONNA DO?

Makeup is like the

wrapping on a

present. You want

it to make a good

first impression, but

the focus should be

on your content . . .

your inner beauty.

There's more to your

package than fancy

bows and paper!

Keep your makeup soft, light, and natural.

When applying eyeshadow, avoid angles or strong lines that draw attention to the eye or look like masking.

Avoid heavy liner. Apply either no line or a smudged line.

Focus on enhancing and not covering up.

Don't use colors that attract the eye and distract from the real you.

Darken lashes with mascara, but don't overdo it.

Don't overtweeze brows or alter lines too much. Make them clean and neat.

Use colors that lift your healthy appearance, rather than hurt it.

Don't live in front of the mirror dealing with every detail. Work on it, then walk away and enjoy your day!

DO-IT-YOURSELF EXTREME MAKEOVER

9 STEPS TO INNER BEAUTY

The Bible contains a simple nine-part makeover secret that will enhance the beauty of any woman. You see, good things aren't naturally a part of the human being. We tend to be selfish, rude, and unkind automatically. But when Christ lives in us, the Holy Spirit can do the makeover for us when we let him.

TRY THIS FRUIT SMOOTHIE!

INGREDIENTS:

Love

Joy

Peace

Patience

Kindness

Goodness

Faithfulness

Gentleness

Self-Control

DIRECTIONS:

Combine generous portions of all these ingredients from Galatians 5:22-23. Take this smoothie with you wherever you go—when you're at school, with your family, or hanging out with your friends!

INNER BEAUTY MAKEOVER: BEFORE AND AFTER

ARE YOU MISSING A FEW INGREDIENTS?

LOVE. The self-sacrificing variety. It's not dependent on anything from the other person.

1. Your sister treats you badly. She yells at you, puts you down when she's with her friends, and doesn't share any of her clothes. She asks you to lend her $10. What do you do?
   a) Tell her off.
   b) Lend her $10, but hold it over her head until she's 30.
   c) Lend her $10, remembering the times other people have shown you love.

JOY. Deep and abiding inner rejoicing given by God no matter what's happening.

2. Your girlfriends all have dates most Friday nights, and you don't. How do you respond?
   a) You find a guy to go out with just to feel better about yourself.
   b) You stay home and feel sorry for yourself.
   c) You still don't like the situation, but you choose to look at the positives instead.

PEACE. Inner peace and quietness, even in the face of tough circumstances; it goes beyond what makes human sense.

3. Your dad lost his job, and your family is going through a rough time financially. How do you react?
   a) You go to school and cry on your friend's shoulder.
   b) You internalize everything and worry constantly.
   c) Underneath the stress, you have an inner peace and can turn your anxieties into prayers.

PATIENCE. You suffer right along with others while they're working out some personal difficulties. You keep being good to them, even when they do wrong to you. You don't try to retaliate for wrong treatment.

4. Your friend is constantly bragging about how much better her clothes are and how much better she is than others. How do you respond to her?
   a) You try to outclass, outrank, and outbrag her.
   b) You make fun of her with your other friends when she's not around.
   c) You listen patiently and make a note to yourself not to talk to your friends like that.

KINDNESS. You show gentleness and kindness that is useful or serviceable.

5. You are out with your friends at the mall. You hear someone call your name, and you look to see another classmate who is handicapped and not well liked by the more popular crowd. What do you do?
   a) You join the group of people who are snickering and pointing in her direction.
   b) You ignore her to try to save face with your friends.
   c) You go out of your way to talk to her, even though you're not sure how the rest of your friends will respond.

GOODNESS. You reach out to others to do good even when it is not deserved.

6. You've been made fun of by someone in your youth group.

She's loud and makes sure everyone hears. One day you arrive to find her crying and pushing others away. What's your reaction?

a) You give her back some of what she deserves and make sure everyone else knows she's crying.

b) You smirk on the inside and decide that no matter what upset her, she probably deserved it.

c) You take the high road and try to comfort her.

FAITHFULNESS. You are trustworthy and reliable.

7. You know you're supposed to be a Christian witness wherever you are. But you're in gym class with two girls you don't know who are telling crude jokes. How do you respond?

a) You throw in an off-color joke yourself to fit in.

b) You laugh with them so you won't seem weird.

c) You stay true to what you believe and try to redirect the conversation.

GENTLENESS. You are humble, meek, and submissive to God's Word.

8. You invite a non-Christian friend to accompany you with several of your "Christian" friends to a youth outing. On the way, your "Christian" friends don't act much like Christians. What's your reaction?

a) You blow up at them in front of the whole group.

b) You whine to your youth leader.

c) You gently confront them in private.

SELF-CONTROL. You control your passions, desires, and impulses.

9. You really like clothes. No amount is too much as far as you're concerned. You just read in the Bible how God wants us to be content, but as you're passing through the mall, you notice a big sale at your favorite store. What do you do?

a) You justify your clothing purchases by spending only as much as your friends spend.

b) You pick out the clothes you want and ask your parents to get them for your birthday.

c) You decide to keep on walking past the store.

SHE SPEAKS

LEIGH (19)

I felt the least pretty after I lost my purity. I thought that was what I wanted. [My boyfriend] made me feel special and beautiful. But after that, I felt like the dirtiest person on earth. I wondered how God could love me ever again. I had made the commitment through True Love Waits. I had broken my promise to my family, my future husband, and God. It made me feel ugly inside.

But I felt prettier than I ever have when I asked God to forgive me for my sin. I stopped having sex with my boyfriend, and eventually I broke up with him. God seemed to say to me, "I have something amazing for you, and this ISN'T it!"

God has forgiven me. Now I'm stressing the inward—like my thoughts that are praiseworthy and noble to God and not to the world. And that's beautiful!

God has something amazing for you too. Dare to trust him. Dare to be faithful to him. Dare to discover his truths regarding the beauty lies you've believed.

And if you do, nobody's going to believe the before and after shots.

NOW THAT'S DOWNRIGHT BEAUTIFUL!

BETHANY DILLON knows about the pressures you face when it comes to beauty—because she faces those same pressures herself. "I'm not singing about being 15 five years ago. I am 15," she says. Bethany has a passion for helping women see themselves as the truly beautiful creations God has made them to be. "I want women to know that God has placed a crown of beauty on their head." Now here's a SHE who really gets it![7]

BEAUTIFUL
BETHANY DILLON

I was so unique
Now I feel skin deep
I count on the makeup to cover it all
Crying myself to sleep 'cause I cannot keep
    their attention
I thought I could be strong
But it's killing me

Does someone hear my cry?
I'm dying for new life

[Chorus]
I want to be beautiful
Make you stand in awe
Look inside my heart,
and be amazed
I want to hear you say
Who I am is quite enough
Just want to be worthy of love
And beautiful

Sometimes I wish I was someone other
    than me
Fighting to make the mirror happy
Trying to find whatever is missing
Won't you help me back to glory?

[Chorus]

You make me beautiful
You make me stand in awe
You step inside my heart, and I am amazed
I love to hear You say
Who I am is quite enough
You make me worthy of love and beautiful

SHEism: A truly beautiful SHE is a girl who sees her value as the whole package—through her inward as well as her outward beauty.

SHE IS PURE

PURE MIND + PURE MOUTH + PURE MOTIVES =
PURE ACTIONS (& HEALTHY YOU!)

*God has called us to live holy lives, not
impure lives. Therefore, anyone who
refuses to live by these rules is not disobeying human teaching but is rejecting
God, who gives his Holy Spirit to you.*
1 Thessalonians 4:7-8

JENNIFER GREW UP IN A CHRISTIAN HOME, but her parents divorced when she was young. She felt cheated and hurt as she watched other girls her age enjoy their relationship with their dad.

FROM AN EARLY AGE, Jennifer loved God. She attended church and completed Bible studies at home. She listened to Christian music, wore Christian T-shirts, and read Christian books. Jennifer even signed a True Love Waits pledge to stay sexually pure until marriage. And she refused to read and watch and say things that she felt displeased God.

THEN CAME MIDDLE SCHOOL. Her family moved, and Jennifer struggled to find her place among her peers. The price for fitting in with other girls was watching movies she thought she'd never watch, saying things she thought she'd never say, and going places she thought she'd never go.

AT LAST SHE FIT IN. Then she met a boy. He told her she was pretty and smart. Jennifer found the daily affirmation from him she'd missed from her dad. One day at age 14, she found herself in bed with her boyfriend. Then he was gone.

SHE MET SOMEONE ELSE, and she found herself in bed with him.

AND THEN SHE MET ANOTHER.

AND ANOTHER.

JENNIFER NOW WRESTLES WITH HPV.

WHAT'S HPV? you may be wondering. Let's put it this way: It's short for human papillomavirus—the most common sexually transmitted disease in the United States. It hits more than 5.5 million people each year. It has no cure. It can cause genital warts and cervical cancer.

JENNIFER WISHES LIFE CAME WITH AN "UNDO" BUTTON. But it doesn't. She recently told her mother, "I've gone too far. I don't know how to get back."

SHE GETS PERSONAL

- Do you find yourself in compromising situations with guys?
- Do you have trouble believing that God has your best interests at heart with the sex rules he established, or do you feel he's trying to keep you from having fun?
- Do you believe sexual purity is a myth and impossible for you to obtain?
- Do you look at guys in a sexual way?
- Do you feel that since you've fallen in the past, there's no point in trying to be pure again?
- Do you masturbate?
- Do you dress immodestly so guys will pay attention to you?
- Do you struggle with impure thoughts?
- Do you expose your mind to images on the computer you shouldn't be looking at?
- Are you toying with the idea of getting involved sexually with someone?

WHAT'S THE **BIG DEAL?**

So you've heard this before . . . your health teacher gives you all the warnings about STDs, your parents get on your case about not going too far with guys, and you're pretty sure you don't want to sign up for teen motherhood. But has anyone ever given you a *real* reason—an at-the-core-of-your-being reason—to save your purity?

God created you, and he knows how you work. He created sex and the rules for sex. He knows what's best for you, and he made those rules to protect you. It's true that when you stay pure you avoid a lot of negative consequences—diseases, heartbreak, pregnancy. But did you know there are also *positive* consequences when you choose to stay pure?

→ You reflect part of God's character: his purity. "Be holy because I am holy" (Leviticus 11:45).

→ You learn to develop healthy relationships with guys. "Respect everyone, and love your Christian brothers and sisters" (1 Peter 2:17).

→ You will have a wedding gift for your future husband no money could ever buy. "A man . . . is joined to his wife, and the two are united into one" (Matthew 19:5).

→ You have a living testimony of how God is working in you. "Be an example to all believers . . . in the way you live, in your love, your faith, and your purity" (1 Timothy 4:12).

SEX IS A BIG DEAL TO GOD BECAUSE *YOU* ARE A BIG DEAL TO GOD.

Run from sexual sin! No other sin so clearly affects the body as this one does. For sexual immorality is a sin against your own body. Don't you realize that your body is the temple of the Holy Spirit, who lives in you and was given to you by God? You do not belong to yourself, for God bought you with a high price. So you must honor God with your body.
1 Corinthians 6:18-20

Let's say you saved up all your cash and bought that really expensive prom dress you've had your eye on for months. If you loaned it to your friend for the dance at her school, you'd expect her to take care of it, right? To remember it's *your* dress, treat it extra-carefully, that kind of thing. Well, you've been bought for a way higher price—the price of Christ's blood. So really our body belongs to God—it's sort of on loan to us for a while. So God expects us to follow his plan for sex—not because he wants to stifle our fun, but because he created it for a special purpose.

If you are feeling hopeless because you've already given your purity away, God is a God of second chances. You may not be able to go back to exactly how things used to be, but God can give you a fresh start. "Look, I am making everything new!" (Revelation 21:5).

Whether you've kept this rule and want strategies for staying pure or you've broken it and want to build standards that will keep you from compromising again, SHE cannot be healthy without being pure.

GiRL TALK!

Get together with a few of your friends. Find a plastic cup from the kitchen and take turns spitting in the cup. Anybody feel inspired to take a drink from the community spittoon? (We didn't think so!)

TALK ABOUT IT: When you have sex with someone, you have sex with every other person your partner has had sex with.

Has it been a long time since you played with Play-Doh? Spend a little dough and buy some dough—Play-Doh, that is. Divide the dough so that each of you has a specific color. Take your Play-Doh and hand it to the person next to you and mix your colors together. Have her do the same thing with the person beside her and so on until the last person holds the whole multicolored mess. Now try to separate the colors to their original purity.

TALK ABOUT IT: Once you have sex with someone, you give something away that can never be gotten back. Sex is more than something you *do*, it is part of who you *are*. It's an outward indicator of what's going on inside of you.

· · · · · · · · · · · · ·

From within, out of a person's heart, come evil thoughts, sexual immorality, theft, murder, adultery, greed, wickedness, deceit, lustful desires, envy, slander, pride, and foolishness.
Mark 7:21-22

Temptation comes from our own desires, which entice us and drag us away. These desires give birth to sinful actions. And when sin is allowed to grow, it gives birth to death.
James 1:14-15

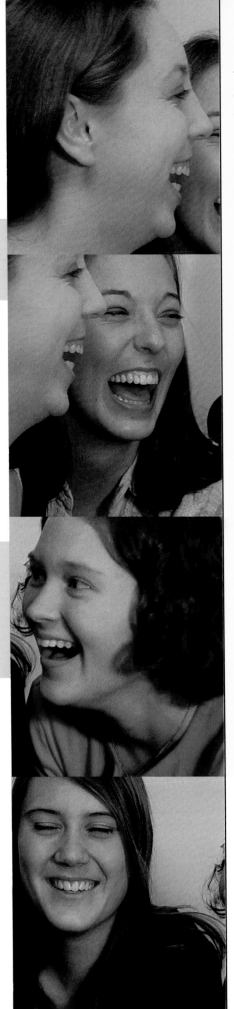

DID YA **KNOW . . .**

The average high school relationship lasts only three weeks after the first sexual experience.[1]

In the United States, more than 65 million people are currently living with an incurable STD.[2]

Each year approximately 4 million American teenagers are infected with an STD.[3]

Young women are biologically more susceptible to chlamydia, gonorrhea, and HIV than any other group of people.[4]

Rates of gonorrhea are highest in females 15–19 years old.[5]

HIV is the eighth leading cause of death among 15- to 24-year-olds in the United States.[6]

In the past decade, sexual experiences among high school students have decreased by 16 percent.[7]

YEAH, BUT . . .

- My boyfriend will break up with me if I don't have sex with him.
- I protect myself.
- All my friends are doing it.
- I've already had sex, so I might as well keep doing it.
- Other:_____

The temptations in your life are no different from what others experience. And God is faithful. He will not allow the temptation to be more than you can stand. When you are tempted, he will show you a way out so that you can endure.
1 Corinthians 10:13

REBECCA SAYS

I have a huge passion for the issue of sexual purity—so much so that I've spoken about it at almost all of my concerts for the past 10 years. It's an issue that spans all marital, economic, and age barriers. I've written a song about it and a book called *Wait for Me*. My passion for this issue is fueled by seeing so many of my generation being ripped off by Satan. He has promoted his lies far too well, and far too few believers are talking about and living the truth that combats those lies. I've spoken to college students in Kyrgyzstan, to a downtown club audience in Paris, and to thousands of people elsewhere around the world about the fact that I'm a virgin and I'm waiting until marriage for sex. Yet I could count on one hand the number of times I've caught any flak for speaking up on this issue. I believe that deep down, most people respect those who stand for purity, and underneath it all, they know it's the right way to go.

"PURITY IS ALWAYS SMART; IMPURITY IS ALWAYS STUPID. NOT SOMETIMES. NOT USUALLY. ALWAYS. . . . THERE ARE NO EXCEPTIONS."

RANDY ALCORN

Fix your thoughts on what is true, and honorable, and right, and pure, and lovely, and admirable. Think about things that are excellent and worthy of praise.
Philippians 4:8

SHE GETS PERSONAL

Who do you feel comfortable talking about sex with?

☐ Your parents

☐ Your friends

☐ Your youth pastor/pastor

☐ Your mentor

Has someone taught you adequately about sex? If so, who was it?

Do you feel your parents have been open to your questions and made it a point to educate you on sex and dating?

Is there anything you wish your parents would have done differently in talking to you about sex?

God blesses those whose hearts are pure, for they will see God.
Matthew 5:8

SHE ASKS

JODY (14)

My mom has never talked with me about sex. Everything I know I've had to learn from my friends. Is there more I can do?

SHE ASKS

BRITTANY (17)

When I make out with my boyfriend, we always seem to go a little further than we did the time before. How far is too far when I'm with my boyfriend?

REBECCA SAYS

I did talk about purity with my mum and dad. From the time my siblings and I were very young, my parents fostered open communication with us. As a teen I felt that I could talk to them about everything, which was such a comfort at that very vulnerable, influential time of life. Our parents were straight with us about the consequences of going against God's way. They also didn't just say, "Don't have sex outside of marriage," but "Here's why God says not to be involved in impurity." This not only made us respect them, but we listened to them too.

For whatever reason, your mom has not been able to talk with you freely about sex. Spend some time together, and without condemning her, share your need to know the truth about sex from someone who loves you. Ask her about her own experiences. Read this chapter together. If this still doesn't work, find a trusted older friend or relative you can talk to about sex. You're asking the right questions, and I'm sure God will honor your search.

REBECCA SAYS

Here are several practical guidelines when it comes to setting physical boundaries. The first thing is for your boyfriend not to touch any part of your body that would be covered by a two-piece bathing suit. Pretty self-explanatory. The second rule is this: Don't let anything that belongs to his body enter anything that belongs to your body. That should about cover it: from sexual intercourse to oral sex to stimulating sex organs. If you think about it, even French kissing is an oral form of intercourse. There are some differences of opinion here, but here's the important question to ask: *Will participating in this activity lead me to do other things that definitely go against my desire for sexual purity?* If you would have a hard time explaining to your future spouse what you did with someone else, then it's probably not a good idea. Be honest with yourself, be honest with your boyfriend, and be honest with God.

SHE'S BEEN THERE

Meet with a trusted, godly woman (such as your mom, your grandma, a family friend, or your youth pastor) and ask her these questions.

• When it comes to dating and sex, would you want me to grow up in the same way you did?

• In what areas would you want things to be different?

• Does society have a different attitude toward sex now than it did when you were growing up?

• What do you wish someone had told you before you started dating?

GIRL TALK!

List the good stuff and the bad stuff from following these rules.

SAFE SEX RULE **USE A CONDOM**

good stuff   bad stuff

GOD'S RULE **SAVE IT FOR MARRIAGE**

good stuff   bad stuff

NO RULE **SEE WHAT HAPPENS**

good stuff   bad stuff

REBECCA SAYS

I once heard a simple talk from the mission director's wife at my church that greatly affected me. She shared that some of the guys at church had complained that they didn't know where to look because of the way many of the girls dressed. It made me see that we have a responsibility to protect guys, especially our Christian brothers.

Several good rules of thumb for our modesty include:

NOT TOO SHORT: Let your arms fall against your body naturally. A good indication of how much your shorts/skirt should cover is where your fingertips reach your legs.

NOT TOO TIGHT: Either buy a larger shirt or layer your clothing so that it's not showing every line of your body.

NOT TOO MUCH SKIN: Cleavage is not meant to be shown! Remember, the more skin you show, the more guys will be tempted to lust.

Keep yourself pure.
1 Timothy 5:22

PURITY WARRIORS

THE GOOD NEWS: YOU *CAN* STAY PURE. God not only gives us rules, but he also provides the means to keep them. Purity is the only way to break sin's cycle of devastation and death and to find wholeness and health.

SEX DOESN'T JUST HAPPEN OUT OF THE BLUE, AND NEITHER DOES PURITY. Though temptation takes place all the time, sexual sin happens only as part of a descending process. A little of this, a little of that. You go here, you look there. You push the boundaries today, and you go a little further tomorrow. One small pleasure combined with one seemingly insignificant compromise, and before you know it, sin has taken over. You may be able to recognize the wrong moves you've made, but can you pinpoint the individual choices that led to them? If you can learn to see and resist the early compromises, you're on your way to preventing the mistakes. Your goal, then, should be to become a good compromise spotter, to stay on your toes, and to defend your purity at all cost.

ONE THING LEADS TO ANOTHER . . .

In order to prevent giving in to sex, you need to understand the steps that lead up to it and the amount of control you have at each step along the way.

FILL IN THE BLANKS BELOW IN ORDER TO SEE THE CLEAR PROGRESSION THAT LEADS TO INTERCOURSE:

1. You think thoughts you know you shouldn't.

2. You listen to things you shouldn't.

3. You go where you shouldn't.

4. You talk to someone you shouldn't.

5. You make a small compromise on your boundaries.

6. You _____.

7. You _____.

8. You _____.

9. You _____.

10. You have sexual intercourse.

Who's in control of the process?

Where can you stop the process?

How can you stop the process?

COLLEEN (17)

Is foreplay wrong, as long as we stop before actual sexual intercourse?

REBECCA SAYS

Foreplay is "mutual sexual stimulation that takes place before intercourse." My opinion is that if what you are doing makes you want to take your clothes off and have sex, then you're walking too close to the fire and you don't need to be there. The other things to remember are:

• God is always watching. Would he be pleased with what you are doing?

• How would you feel if this person turned out to be someone else's future husband and not yours?

• Would you be embarrassed to tell your future children about what you are doing?

Remembering these questions will help keep you out of the danger zone.

How can a young person stay pure? By obeying your word.
Psalm 119:9

*Run from sexual sin!
No other sin so clearly affects
the body as this one does.
For sexual immorality
is a sin against your own body.*
1 Corinthians 6:18

FAQs FREQUENTLY ASKED QUESTIONS

IS ORAL SEX REALLY SEX?
THE SHORT ANSWER: YES.

Dr. Peter Leone (University of North Carolina at Chapel Hill) says: Oral sex is sex "because it's genital contact—that's it. If something involves how people feel about themselves sexually, and it involves sex organs, then it's sex."[8]

WHAT IS ORAL SEX GOING TO COST ME?
YOU CAN GET STD'S THROUGH ORAL SEX.

Here are just a few examples:

- Syphilis: Can lead to brain damage. Blindness. Paralysis. Dementia. Death.
- Chlamydia: Can cause pelvic inflammatory disease. Infertility.
- Gonorrhea: Can lead to pelvic inflammatory disease. Infertility. Death.
- HIV: Causes AIDS. No cure. Fatal.

YOU CAN GET EMOTIONALLY BURNED THROUGH ORAL SEX.

Here are just a few ways:

- Guilt. Rejection. Loss. Shame. Confusion. Heartbreak.
- Any act of touching someone else's genitals is sex! And sex outside marriage is sin. Always has been, always will be.

WHAT ARE GOD'S RULES ABOUT SEX?

- **MARRIED SEX:** Sex is *good* when it's between a husband and a wife. God designed sex for us to enjoy. "A man leaves his father and mother and is joined to his wife, and the two are united into one" (Genesis 2:24).

- **PREMARITAL SEX:** Sex is *not good* before you're married. "We must not engage in sexual immorality" (1 Corinthians 10:8).

- **ADULTERY:** Sex is *not good* with someone other than your husband. "You must not commit adultery" (Mark 10:19).

- **HOMOSEXUALITY:** Sex is *not good* with someone who's the same gender. "Don't you realize that those who do wrong will not inherit the Kingdom of God? Don't fool yourselves. Those who indulge in sexual sin, or who worship idols, or commit adultery, or are male prostitutes, or practice homosexuality, or are thieves, or greedy people, or drunkards, or are abusive, or cheat people—none of these will inherit the Kingdom of God" (1 Corinthians 6:9-10).

SHE
ASKS

9 STEPS YOU CAN TAKE TO STAY PURE

There's a story in the Bible you won't believe. It was written over 3,000 years ago, but it could just as easily happen today. Even though the main character is a man, the purity struggle is something that applies to us women too.

While I was at the window of my house,
  looking through the curtain,
I saw some naive young men,
  and one in particular who lacked
    common sense.
He was crossing the street near the house
  of an immoral woman,
  strolling down the path by her house.
It was at twilight, in the evening,
  as deep darkness fell.
The woman approached him,
  seductively dressed and sly of heart.
She was the brash, rebellious type,
  never content to stay at home.
She is often in the streets and markets,
  soliciting at every corner.

She threw her arms around him
  and kissed him,
  and with a brazen look she said,
"I've just made my peace offerings
  and fulfilled my vows.
You're the one I was looking for!
  I came out to find you, and here
    you are!
My bed is spread with beautiful blankets,
  with colored sheets of Egyptian linen.
I've perfumed my bed
  with myrrh, aloes, and cinnamon.
Come, let's drink our fill of love until
  morning.
  Let's enjoy each other's caresses,
for my husband is not home.
  He's away on a long trip.

He has taken a wallet full of money
  with him
  and won't return until later this
    month."
So she seduced him with her pretty
  speech
  and enticed him with her flattery.
He followed her at once,
  like an ox going to the slaughter.
He was like a stag caught in a trap,
  awaiting the arrow that would
    pierce its heart.
He was like a bird flying into a snare,
  little knowing it would cost him his
    life.
Proverbs 7:6-23

I. BE WISE.

"... naive young men ... who lacked common sense..."

Know what you will and will not do ahead of time. Recognize temptation before it gets too big for you to handle. Your first line of defense against impurity: your running shoes! "Run from sexual sin" (1 Corinthians 6:18).

REBECCA SAYS

I maintain a "shoe in the door" policy with guys I date. If circumstances are such that we happen to be in a room alone together, I literally put a shoe in the door to prop it open. This way we both know that someone could walk in at any minute. Though taking this stand has not been easy at times, it has helped me in my effort to live above reproach. Dating only Christian men and keeping accountability people in my life are other biblical boundaries that I adhere to without exception.

2. DON'T GO WHERE YOU SHOULDN'T GO.

"... crossing the street near the house of an immoral woman ..."

Are there parties you know you shouldn't go to? Are there hangouts where you'll fall back into your old (bad) habits? Don't go there! Some girls don't physically go where they shouldn't go, but their

minds and emotions do. They think and daydream themselves to places they don't belong. Don't go where you shouldn't—emotionally and physically!

WHAT ABOUT YOU?

Where have you gone physically or emotionally that made you feel dirty and compromised?

....

....

What was it about the temptation that first got your attention?

....

....

How will you avoid going there again?

....

....

....

3. STAY IN THE LIGHT.

"It was at twilight, in the evening, as deep darkness fell."

If it has to be done in the dark when no one is watching, it's wrong!

QUICK QUESTIONS

If you're about to do something with your boyfriend and it feels wrong, it probably is. Before you do anything, ask yourself:

- Would I do this at Starbucks?
  ☐ yes ☐ no

- Would I do this if my youth pastor or my little sister was sitting in the room?
  ☐ yes ☐ no

- Does this act bring me closer to God?
  ☐ yes ☐ no

4. BE ABLE TO SPOT SIN'S MANY DISGUISES.

". . . seductively dressed and sly of heart . . ."

Arm yourself with what is right so you will know wrong when it comes. Know the truth so you'll call the lies for what they are. Temptation is kinda like those plastic desserts they have on display at some restaurants—do you know which ones we're talking about? They look enticing on the outside, but one bite and you realize looks aren't everything. Satan likes to wrap sin and lies into pretty packages—but the consequences are more deadly than a mouthful of plastic.

5. DON'T HANG OUT WITH THE WRONG PEOPLE.

". . . the brash, rebellious type, never content to stay at home . . . often in the streets and markets, soliciting at every corner . . ."

Choose Christian friends who challenge you to step your faith up a notch, not friends who drag you down.

"If you play in the mud with white gloves on, the gloves always get muddy, the mud never gets 'glovey.'"

CHUCK SWINDOLL

Name three people you have hung out with when you shouldn't have. What effect did it have on you?

1 ....

....

2 ....

....

3 ....

....

6. DRAW YOUR LINES CAREFULLY (AND STICK TO 'EM).

". . . threw her arms around him and kissed him, and with a brazen look she said, . . . 'You're the one I was looking for!'"

Draw the solid line of what you will and won't do. Talk to your now-boyfriend or your someday-boyfriend about the boundaries you have set. Then walk that line carefully. Put yourself only in situations where you can uphold the standards you've set for yourself.

Stuff I will do	Stuff I will not do under any circumstances

My line

7. DON'T LET YOURSELF GET WORN DOWN.

"My bed is spread with beautiful blankets, with colored sheets of Egyptian linen. I've perfumed my bed with myrrh, aloes, and cinnamon."

You're most vulnerable when you're tired, lonely, depressed, angry, or struggling in a relationship. Satan even tried this tactic on Jesus. "When the devil had finished tempting Jesus, he left him until the next opportunity came" (Luke 4:13). Satisfy yourself with Christ, then sin will seem less attractive (see John 6:35). When you get into a situation and you are no longer sure of what's right, follow this battle plan:

- Retreat! Get out of the dangerous situation.

- Go to the top. Ask God for help.

- Find an ally. Ask a friend or mentor to keep you accountable.

- Regroup. Come up with a plan to avoid a close call like this in the future.

8. DON'T BELIEVE EVERYONE'S DOING IT.

"Come, let's drink our fill of love until morning. Let's enjoy each other's caresses."

Sex outside God's plan has consequences: unplanned pregnancy, STDs, destroyed reputations, emotional pain. Don't be duped into believing that no one will know.

You may be sure that your sin will find you out.
Numbers 32:23
Those who follow crooked paths will slip and fall.
Proverbs 10:9

But even if no one did find out, the most important audience would know: your Father who sees all. "He watches everyone closely, examining every person on earth" (Psalm 11:4).

When it comes to sex, statistics say that everybody is *not* doing it. In fact, purity is on the rise. The percentage of high school students who said they'd had sexual intercourse dropped from 54 percent in 1991 to 47 percent in 2003.[9]

But even if everyone else *were* doing it, the Bible tells us that when we follow a blind man, he'll lead us into a ditch (Matthew 15:14). If we follow a blind culture, it will lead us to destruction.

GIRL TALK!

Think of at least three people who stand for the same things you do when it comes to purity. Get together with them and make an agreement to hold each other accountable for making your rules on sex and keeping these rules.

- What accountability questions will you ask each other when you're not dating anyone?

- What accountability questions will you ask each other when you're considering dating a guy?

- What accountability questions will you ask when you're going out with someone?

9. KNOW A TRAP WHEN YOU SEE ONE.

"She seduced him with her pretty speech and enticed him with her flattery. He followed her at once, like an ox going to the slaughter. He was like a stag caught in a trap, awaiting the arrow that would pierce its heart. He was like a bird flying into a snare, little knowing it would cost him his life."

SHE'S BEEN THERE

Ask a trusted, godly woman (such as your mom, your grandma, a family friend, or your youth pastor) about some regrets she's had in her relationships with guys. What have these regrets meant in her life?

Together, think about some girls you know who've gone too far and the consequences that have resulted.

Talk about people you know who've made purity their goal and the blessings that have resulted in their life.

THE BUZZ ON A BIBLE **HE**

JOSEPH

TALK ABOUT SIBLING RIVALRY: Joseph had a less than perfect life. When he was 17, his jealous brothers decided to get rid of him once and for all. They stole the cool coat his dad had given him, and they sold him to some Ishmaelite traders. He was taken to Egypt and sold as a slave to Potiphar, captain of Pharoah's palace guard.

THE LURE: His hard work was noticed and rewarded by Potiphar, who gave Joseph prestigious positions in his household. His "work" was also noticed by Mrs. Potiphar. Apparently Joseph was "handsome and well-built" (Genesis 39:6), and she tried to get him to sleep with her. Joseph faced a moment of decision. He could resist her advances, or he could enjoy the compliment of this woman's attention and accept her offer. After all, no one would know. No one would get hurt. No one would blame him for seeking a little harmless affection.

WOULD HE OR WOULDN'T HE? Joseph didn't stand around doing eeny-meeny-miney-moe trying to decide what he would do. He'd already set his standards. He'd drawn his lines. He knew God's rules, and he lived by them. So Joseph refused. Immediately. Period.

WHY NOT? "My master trusts me" (39:8).
"It would be a great sin against God" (39:9).

TEMPTATION IS A STALKER: But the woman kept pressuring, and Joseph kept resisting by staying out of her way as much as he could. One day she grabbed him by his shirt and demanded that he give in. Joseph tore himself away, leaving his shirt behind.

PURITY PAYS: The woman lied and used Joseph's shirt to say he'd tried to rape her. He landed in prison. Where was God? Why didn't he reward Joseph for keeping God's rules?
But even in prison the Lord was with Joseph. After a period of time, Joseph's name was cleared, and God used him to accomplish great things for God's Kingdom—including saving the family line Jesus would be born into.
Purity brings blessings.
Impurity brings curses.

WANT MORE DETAILS? For the whole scoop, check out Genesis 39.

SHEism:

The truly pure SHE keeps her heart clean before God and enjoys the health of a pure mind and body.

SHE SPEAKS

TAMARA (18)

I was in the sixth grade when I met Stacie at the small Christian school we attended. I thought she was so pretty, and it amazed me how she could attract so many guys both at school and at church. One night at her house, I shared with her my commitment to purity. She told me that it would be nice if she could remain a virgin until her wedding night, but she doubted if she could save herself until then. I explained that God would help us in our relationships, but she seemed to think she would be fine on her own.

The years passed and Stacie and I grew apart. At 16, she had finally found someone special. She informed everyone how hot her new boyfriend was and how special he made her feel. Several weeks later, Stacie told me that she had lost her virginity. As a Christian, I felt like I should have done something more to make her realize how important purity really was. I wanted to tell her that God wanted this to be a time when she longed for more of his love, not superficial love that only lasted as long as her boyfriend's hormones were satisfied.

After high school graduation, I saw Stacie again. She was dating a different guy and found herself pregnant with his baby. She asked about my plans for college in the fall, then she talked about how good my life seemed to her.

It was then that I realized the power of purity and that God's intention for intimacy was to be shared only with a spouse. This girl who was constantly surrounded by boys wanted the life of someone who never even had a boyfriend. Someone who seemingly had everything longed for *my* life. I realized all over again that what we need is not a temporary physical arousal, but a permanent spiritual awakening.

God's will is for you to be holy, so stay away from all sexual sin. Then each of you will control his own body and live in holiness and honor.
1 Thessalonians 4:3-4

REBECCA SAYS

Sometimes after a concert in which I've spoken about sexual purity, I've had people say, "Thanks for speaking to the girls about sexual purity." I generally reply by reminding them with a smile that my message is not just for girls but for guys too!

The idea that purity is only a female issue doesn't fly with God either. Guys are just as responsible for their actions before him as girls are. On page 112, we read about a Bible HE who was fully committed to purity—a wonderful example for those of us who want to be part of SHE-dom.

THE WORD ON DATING/COURTING

- Date/court only Christians (see 2 Corinthians 6:14).

- Hang out with people who live by your principles (see 1 Corinthians 15:33).

- Plan the entire date in advance, with no gaps (see Ecclesiastes 3:5).

- Be accountable to someone about your purity (see Proverbs 24:26).

- Remember God is with you on your dates (see Jeremiah 16:17).

- Write out your own rules and enforce them yourself. Never think it's someone else's responsibility (see Galatians 6:4-5).

- Don't do anything with your date you wouldn't want someone else doing with your future mate (see Matthew 7:12).

PURITY COVENANT

A MAN NAMED JOB MADE THIS PROMISE ABOUT HIS OWN SEXUAL PURITY:

*I made a covenant with my eyes
not to look with lust at a young woman.*
JOB 31:1

I want to make a commitment on this day to become and remain a pure woman:

- I will speak and act purely.

- I will dress modestly.

- I will take captive any impure or lustful thoughts.

- I will keep myself from watching, listening to, and looking at anything that would have a harmful impact on my mind and life.

- I will not participate in any form of sex outside of marriage.

- I will pray for God's power to remain true to this covenant.

_____   _____
Signature   Date

_____
Witness

Run from anything that stimulates youthful lusts. Instead, pursue righteous living, faithfulness, love, and peace. Enjoy the companionship of those who call on the Lord with pure hearts.
2 Timothy 2:22

SHE IS FREE

YOU DON'T HAVE TO LIVE IN BONDAGE. GOD CAN MAKE YOU HEALTHY AND FREE!

Who will free me from this life that is dominated by sin and death? Thank God! The answer is in Jesus Christ our Lord.
Romans 7:24-25

Let's go back in time for a minute. The year is 1925. The location: Cave City, Kentucky. Our "hero": a farmer named Floyd Collins, who is die-hard into caving. One day in January he sets out to Sand Cave, hoping to find a new opening to the Mammoth Caves. Everything is going fine for the first 70 feet or so. But then it happens. A 27-pound chunk of limestone breaks off and pins his leg in a narrow crack. Collins is trapped. And alone. With no way out.

After 24 hours, rescuers find him and try everything to get him out. A reporter even gets close enough to talk to him and pass him coffee and milk. But the rocks prove to be an unforgiving opponent. Eighteen days later, Collins is finally pulled out. He's dead, only inches from freedom.

Experts in the years since have tried to figure out what went wrong in Collins's journey. They pinpointed two key mistakes:

1. HE DIDN'T CARRY APPROPRIATE SOURCES OF LIGHT.

2. HE WENT ALONE.[1]

So maybe you're not planning to go caving any time soon (the bats alone would be reason enough for us to keep our distance!). But we can learn a few things about freedom from our friend Floyd. When you face the places in your life that threaten to trap you and pin you down, don't try to make it without your true Light source. And don't try to go it alone. Okay?

DAWN (19)

I found freedom after I started obeying my Christian parents again. I broke up with the guy who'd gotten me pregnant, and I felt free from all of the garbage that was holding me down. I didn't have to keep secrets from my parents anymore. Most of all, I was able to be close and real with God again. That was really freeing—just knowing that I was honoring God in my actions. I always felt like I was in bondage when I was going through the rebellious stuff. I felt like part of me was trying to get freedom, but Satan was trying to destroy me and keep me from being free.

FAQs FREQUENTLY ASKED QUESTIONS

WHAT IS BONDAGE?

BONDAGE: a chain around your head to keep you from envisioning a hopeful future

BONDAGE: a chain around your feet to keep you from changing direction

BONDAGE: a chain around your hands to keep you from breaking free

BONDAGE: anything that keeps you from experiencing God's best for you

YEAH, BUT . . .

1. Everyone has baggage.
2. Bad things happen. We can't change our circumstances.
3. I can't control what other people do.
4. My genes determine who I am.
5. I have a right to feel any way I want to feel.
6. Other:_____

HANG ON A SEC—DON'T SKIP THIS CHAPTER!
You might be thinking freedom isn't an issue for you. After all, you live in a free country. You can decide who to marry, which college to go to, and which church to attend. But being free is about more than voting rights or no curfew. It's about getting rid of the stuff that ties you down, holds you back, locks you up. And it means getting rid of that stuff for good.

HOW DOES BONDAGE SNAG YOU?
You may be in bondage and not know it.

You may have gotten so used to being in bondage that it feels natural.

You may have accepted that your bondage will never change.

Describe how freedom—or the lack of it—affects your life right now.

IN YOUR RELATIONSHIPS:

IN YOUR SPIRITUAL LIFE:

IN YOUR THOUGHTS/EMOTIONS:

SHE ASKS

ALLIE (17)

When I was 13, I was raped by a guy who lived next door to us. I'll hate him until the day I die.

REBECCA SAYS

It grieves me to hear your story and the stories of other girls I've met on the road who have faced such horrible abuse and mistreatment. And if it hurts me like that, how much greater God *must* hurt with you and long to love you as a father embraces a hurting child. You are SO loved, my sister!

The problem with unresolved pain and unforgiveness is that it rots us from the inside out. Like a cancerous tumor that *eats away* inside us, without treatment it begins to grow and take over our body—eventually bringing death. Don't let the enemy rip you off even more than he already has. Bring your pain into the light and let God heal you on the inside.

Sin is no longer your master, for you no longer live under the requirements of the law. Instead, you live under the freedom of God's grace.
Romans 6:14

GET OUT OF JAIL FREE QUIZ

Are you really free? Answer these ten questions to find out!

yes	no		
☐	☐	1.	Do you struggle to let go of the past?
☐	☐	2.	Do you have trouble forgiving others, yourself, or God for certain things that have happened to you?
☐	☐	3.	Do you fear what might happen in the future?
☐	☐	4.	Are you afraid of letting other people see the real you?
☐	☐	5.	Do you allow one or more habits to control you?
☐	☐	6.	Do you ever lie or cheat?
☐	☐	7.	Do you often feel sad or depressed?
☐	☐	8.	Do you stay busy so you won't have to deal with difficult issues?
☐	☐	9.	Do you resist quietness and alone time?
☐	☐	10.	Do you get angry easily?

If you answered *yes* to any of these questions, you might not be as free as you thought you were. Go back over the questions and list the problem areas. How can you start tackling one of those now?

....

....

....

....

FREEDOM **FROM THE TOP**

When Jesus spoke these words, most people—including many who believed in him—didn't realize he wanted to take their heart-cuffs off and free them from everything that kept them from discovering the full life he came to bring them. Because they didn't see themselves as trapped, they also didn't see their need to be set free, so they missed out on the joy, peace, hope, and love he offered.

But Jesus wasn't talking about freedom as in human rights or politics. It wasn't the kind of freedom our nation's forefathers fought for. It was an even bigger sort of freedom—the kind our heavenly Father gave his Son to die for. Jesus-brand freedom lets us hand over our "right" to hold on to things and allow him to give us back the kinds of

[Jesus said:]
"You will know the truth,
and the truth
will set you free. . . .
If the Son sets you free,
you are truly free."
John 8:32, 36

freedoms that can never change or be taken away. Jesus-brand freedom helps us face the disappointments and heartbreaks of life and choose to respond in the healthy and loving way that Jesus wou Jesus-brand freedom gives us healing a strength to move past our old hurts. An reassures us of his love for us for alway

Life is messy. There's no getting around that. You will always have areas your life where Satan tries to attack yo heart-cuff you, and trash your freedom

But even though you're left with stuff to deal with from time time, God can turn any roadblock into a doorway to freedom Our job is to recognize the truth, which sets us free. And we need to be able to identify the thieves that try to steal our freedom.

DID YA KNOW . . .

One in four girls in middle school and high school is involved in self-mutilation—cutting her skin until it bleeds. Those who do it call an addiction, a way to relieve stress.[2]

Suicide is the third leading cause of death among people ages 15 to 24.[3]

Every day in the United States, more than 3,000 people under 18 become a slave to cigarettes.[4]

In a nationwide survey, 17 out of 100 students reported carrying a weapon to school at least once in the past 30 days.[5]

One in four adolescent girls has symptoms of depression.[6]

 SPEAKS

STACY (16)

I've grown up in a Christian home. I've been free, but I haven't felt free. I have felt chained down to the world. It's the total opposite of freedom. It's weird to think about.

 SPEAKS

EMILY (15)

I know the right words to say. I even know the right verses to quote. But when I'm honest with myself, I'm not who I make everyone think I am. Instead, I'm hiding the things I don't want them to know.

 SPEAKS

ROBIN (19)

I felt like I had two different lives going on. On the one hand, I was staying out with my friends all night drinking and doing all kinds of stuff. Some Saturday nights I would do that, then go to church on Sunday morning It took a lot of energy trying to keep up with these two different lifestyles. It was very confusing at times.

I have swept away your sins like a cloud. I have scattered your offenses like the morning mist. Oh, return to me, for I have paid the price to set you free.
Isaiah 44:22

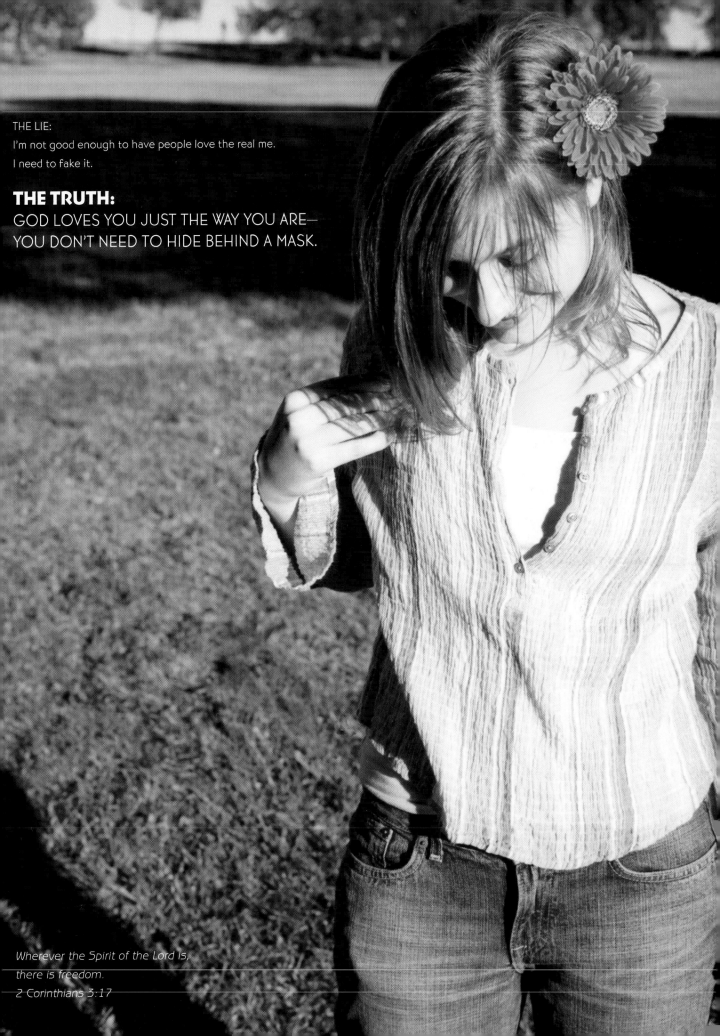

THE LIE:
I'm not good enough to have people love the real me.
I need to fake it.

THE TRUTH:
GOD LOVES YOU JUST THE WAY YOU ARE—
YOU DON'T NEED TO HIDE BEHIND A MASK.

Wherever the Spirit of the Lord is,
there is freedom.
2 Corinthians 3:17

FREEDOM THIEF #1: THE FAKER

The Faker teaches you how to wear different masks to hide the real you. You wear your spiritual mask to church and your cool mask with your friends. And you'll do almost anything to make other people think you've got it all together.

The Faker. He is a first-class freedom thief. He likes to attack us girls more than the guys, and he knows one of our weak spots: our self-esteem. The Faker works hard on the inside of you to convince you that you're not good enough and need to be somebody different. What does that mean? Insecurities. And lots of them.

HAS THE FAKER FAKED YOU OUT?

1. You are going to a dance at your school on Friday. How do you decide what to wear?
   a) You go through your closet and try things on until you find something that you love. It's comfortable and modest, and you've always thought it looked good on you. It's perfect!
   b) You call your friends to find out what they're wearing to get some ideas for what might be good. Then you scan your stuff until you find something that you think will work.
   c) You make plans to go home with one of your friends earlier in the week. You can find out exactly what she is going to wear so you can wear something similar. Actually, you're hoping to borrow whatever she recommends.

2. Summer vacation is finally here! All your friends have decided to join a soccer team together. But running after balls isn't really your thing; you were kind of hoping to join a community swim team this summer. How do you decide which to do?
   a) You join the swim team. You've been looking forward to it all year. Maybe you can go watch your friends play a game sometime.
   b) You agonize for weeks trying to decide. Should you do what all your friends want? Or should you go for the swim team—what you *really* wanted to try?
   c) You start shopping for cleats. All your friends think it's a great idea, so it's a soccer summer for you!

3. This year you had an agreement with your mom that you would be responsible for practicing the piano daily without her nagging you. And you do practice, maybe three times a week. Okay, sometimes once a week. It doesn't seem like a big deal until your recital. You stumble through the piece, pausing several times and playing wrong notes, and everyone notices. When you get home, your disappointed mom asks what happened.
   a) You admit that you haven't been practicing daily like you promised, apologize, and ask her to remind you sometimes.
   b) You tell her that you have been too busy to practice every day, but you are still practicing. You think it could have gone a little better.
   c) You tell her you don't know. After all, you have been practicing. You blame the teacher for giving you a piece that was too hard or for not giving you enough time to prepare. Besides, it wasn't that bad, was it?

4. Your mom tells you not to touch the cupcakes on the counter because she needs all of them for your brother's birthday party tomorrow. Then she leaves, and you're alone with the cupcakes, warm and fresh, while you were just thinking of a snack. Your older sister gets home from work and helps herself to one—evidently she didn't get the "Don't touch!" memo. She did it first . . . so you do too, eating quickly. But not quickly enough; as you turn back around, you see your mom standing in the doorway.

a) Before she can even say a word, you apologize and ask forgiveness. She did tell you not to touch them. You offer to help her make more.

b) You apologize, but not before telling her that your sister took one and pointing out that she has tons, that you're starving, and that she wouldn't have even noticed if she hadn't caught you.

c) You insist that it was your sister's fault. She took one, so you should be able to too. It's not fair for your mother to blame you and not her anyway!

5 Your youth group is going to be running the church service next week, and your youth leader asks for volunteers for a few things. He needs a few people to lead singing for the congregation, and he needs some others to help out in the nursery. When it's your turn to sign up, you notice that there is only one opening left for singing, but almost no one has agreed to help with the nursery. What do you do?

a) You've been told you're good with kids, and it looks like they really need help there, so you sign up where it looks like you can help out most.

b) You waver back and forth; you know you'll be more useful in the nursery, but people might think you're not helping if they can't see you.

c) You grab the last singing spot. You're only a mediocre singer, but you want people to know how much you serve God—how will they know if you're downstairs out of sight?

6 Your dad breaks his leg one afternoon while painting the garage. He'll be fine, but things are kind of hectic all evening at your house with people running to the hospital and stuff. Just as you and your siblings realize it's way past dinnertime and no one has even thought of what to eat, a neighbor rings the doorbell. She has brought over some dinner for you, and it's good! How do you respond?

a) You thank her as you take it into the house to share with your family. And before you eat you pray, thanking God that your dad wasn't seriously hurt, for the good neighbors he's given you, and for the super dinner.

b) You thank your kind neighbor, then bring in the dinner and say your routine prayer before tearing into it.

c) You eat it as fast as you can and remember the time you and your dad helped her rake her leaves after you did yours. Finally, she's paying you back the favor.

7 Your English class is doing a writing unit, and your teacher asks everyone to write a page introducing themselves. You're supposed to include what activities you like to do, what you are good at, and some of your favorites—food, color, movie, book, etc. The idea is to give your teacher some idea of what you're like.

a) Excited, you start writing down things about yourself as fast as you can. There are so many things you want to say, you're not sure a page will be enough.

b) You get the facts down, telling your teacher what you look like, how old you are, where you live, how many people are in your family. You don't leave much space for your opinions and preferences.

c) You think about your friends and what they will probably write and put those things down. Not quite to the end of the page, you try to guess what the teacher might like to read. You tell her you like writing, and your favorite book just happens to be the last one you read in class. You don't have a favorite color.

8 You've had a weird day. You did great on a test, and a guy you like sat by you at lunch. But you also missed the bus, got hit in the head with a volleyball, and had to walk home in the pouring rain. You don't know if today is terrible or great, and you feel like your emotions are running wild. Then you find out that your little brother "borrowed" your bike, managing to deflate both tires. He feels really bad about it, but you're already angry enough.

a) You take a deep breath and try to think about him too. You're really mad and it's his fault, but you try to forgive him. Or at least not yell at him and make him feel worse.

b) You shout at him without thinking about it, but then try to settle down a bit. Even though you're still upset with him, you know he didn't mean to damage your bike.

c) You take a wild swing at him and start screaming. It's been a crazy day, and you shouldn't have to deal with one more thing. As you run off toward his room to break stuff, you slam the door as hard as you can.

• •

MOSTLY A'S: It looks as if you won't let yourself be faked out! You've done a great job at guarding against lies that you're not good enough as you are. Keep on being bold enough to be yourself and to take responsibility for your own decisions.

MOSTLY B'S: You know what you're like, but sometimes you're tempted to be someone else. Be on your guard against the Faker! Remember that although his lies can be attractive, being your real self is more attractive.

MOSTLY C'S: Hmm, it looks like you may need to take another look at yourself—the Faker may be tricking you into thinking you need to be different. Put away your masks, and don't let others convince you that you're someone you're not! Don't be afraid to do what you know is right.

SHE ASKS

DESTINY (18)

As a pastor's oldest child, I am not for real. Growing up in the church, I live in a glass house. Everyone is watching what I do. If I do something, the whole church knows about it. Sometimes I would do the total opposite because I wanted to prove them wrong—that I'm not perfect. It's hard when people have such high standards that are not humanly possible to achieve. How do I learn to be real and still protect myself?

REBECCA SAYS

I remember during an Australian tour being so exhausted and overwhelmed that I was crying as my opening song was beginning. I had about 30 seconds before I had to go out in front of an audience that was expecting me to be "on top of it." I know the struggle between wanting to be real and living in what feels like a fishbowl. What I have found is that ultimately if I live to please God, he takes care of the rest. None of us are ever going to be able to please everyone. God is the one we must seek to please. Yet we have the assurance that when we do miss the mark, because of his grace he still loves us.

SHAKE THE FAKE

The Faker is not content with just causing you to make a mistake. He makes you think you *are* the mistake! It's time to get at the source of the shame the Faker has caused you. Which is it?

- Shame resulting from others' words

  I feel ashamed because of verbal abuse. I was called names that defined my worth.

  I feel ashamed because someone told me there is something wrong with who I am.

- Shame resulting from others' actions

  I feel ashamed because other people have treated me like I'm no good.

  I feel ashamed because shame was used to make me submissive.

- Shame from constantly being in a poisonous environment

  I feel ashamed because that's how things work in my home.

  I feel ashamed because of something I was taught at an early age.

- Other:_____

IT'S TIME TO REPLACE THE FAKER'S LIES WITH GOD'S TRUTH:

Instead of shame and dishonor, you will enjoy a double share of honor.
You will possess a double portion of prosperity in your land,
and everlasting joy will be yours.
Isaiah 61:7

Draw pictures or symbols to express what this verse means to you.

What is the shame that God longs to change?

What does this verse tell you about what God wants for you?

THE FAKER TELLS YOU:

"You'll never change." "You'll never measure up." "There's something wrong with you." These lies are from Satan, the father of lies and the original Faker.

BUT GOD TELLS YOU:

"I created you in my own image" (see Genesis 1:27). "You are my masterpiece. I created you anew in Christ Jesus, so you can do the good things I planned for you long ago" (see Ephesians 2:10). Those are the truths that God, the loving Father, wants you to know. He wants you to come in from hiding. He wants to make you healthy and free for the wonderful future he has for you. A future where you can be yourself . . . where you can be loved for *you*, both by God and by other people.

FREEDOM THIEF #2:
THE GRUDGE MAKER

Beware of another freedom thief: the Grudge Maker, aka unforgiveness. Grudge Maker follows close behind you, watching and waiting for someone to treat you wrong. Then he begins his game: the instant replay of the hurt over and over again in your mind, building it bigger until you have one monster-sized grudge.

The world tells us: "Seek revenge!" "Get even!" "You deserve payback!" But Jesus put unforgiveness into permanent remix (see Matthew 18:21-35). Here's how the story goes.

1. **You owe a big debt to your Master.**

2. **Your Master forgives all of it.**

3. **Someone owes you a smaller debt.**

4. **You refuse to let him or her off the hook.**

5. **Because of your response, the Master throws you into prison. "That's what my heavenly Father will do to you if you refuse to forgive your brothers and sisters from your heart" (Matthew 18:35).**

3 Things Every Post-Faker Should Hang on Her Fridge

1. **I am loved by God.**
2. **I can be healed.**
3. **I can build a new legacy.**

SHE SPEAKS

JO (15)

[Jo received this letter from a friend of many years, who'd just confessed her sexual addiction.] "Jo, I've never, ever felt so free. This was the worst thing ever, keeping this from you guys and just being chained to it. I couldn't stop it, Jo. I masked it. I hid it from you and from my family well. But I just couldn't stop doing it. Every time we talked in church about not letting Satan get a foothold, I was crushed. I knew I was living in sin and that I couldn't serve two masters. But now, I feel free. And happy. And alive. I'm heartbrokenly free!"

Jesus—your Master—has forgiven you, and now it's time to let go of all the things that have been done to you. It's time to free yourself from the prison of unforgiveness.

THE LIE:
I've been hurt so badly I'll never be able to forgive.

THE TRUTH:
GOD ENABLES US TO FORGIVE,
AND WE WON'T BE FREE
UNTIL WE DO.

Don't worry about anything; instead,
pray about everything. Tell God what you
need, and thank him for all he has done.
Philippians 4:6

SHE'S BEEN THERE

Meet with a trusted, godly woman and start to bust out of unforgiveness prison together.

- Get a piece of paper, a pen, and a lunch bag.
- Cut the piece of paper into strips—a lot of strips if you have a lot to forgive, fewer if you don't.
- Spread the strips of paper in front of you on a table. Close your eyes and pray. Ask God to show you who you need to forgive. As he brings people to mind, write their names on the paper, noting the PERSON and the EVENT.
- Keep writing until all the unforgiveness inside you is down on paper. Pray again for any remaining people you need to forgive.
- Now pick them up one by one. Hold each in your hand and pray something like this:

> ❀ "God, I forgive _____ for _____. I can't do this on my own, but you can do it through me. Thank you for forgiving my sins. I'm letting it go today, once and for all. Thank you, God, because unforgiveness toward this person is not allowed to hold me captive again." ❀

- Now do the same with the next person and event you have to forgive. Keep going until you have prayed about each slip of paper.
- Wad up all the strips you've prayed over and put them in the lunch bag. Then crunch the full bag and watch yourself throw it away.
- Over the next 30 days, keep track of the freedom you feel as you shake the Grudge Maker.

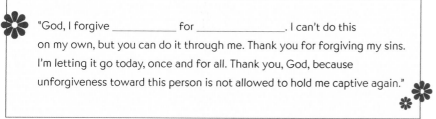

3 Things Every Post-Grudge Maker Should Hang on Her Fridge

1. **God has forgiven me.**
2. **I can forgive others.**
3. **I can let go of the past.**

SHE ASKS

SAVANNAH (16)

I'm a Christian, but I can't forgive my dad for leaving us when I was a little girl.

REBECCA SAYS

A friend of mine told me about the day she was released from the bondage of unforgiveness she had been holding on to against someone who had hurt her deeply. A close friend and mentor said to her, "You are being tormented in a prison of unforgiveness. The things that happened to you all those years ago still have their hold on you. You must forgive this person from your heart for his offenses or you will remain in bondage to him." My friend went on to name every act of betrayal this man had done to her. With everything she mentioned, her friend laid some object on the table—a paper clip, a pencil, a tissue. Then one by one, she picked up the object, named the offense, and prayed to forgive, letting them go once and for all. Her complete healing didn't happen overnight, because she was dealing with years of pain, but gradually she felt her burdens lifted. Offering forgiveness to the person who had wounded her was the beginning of her being set free.

You will never be able to "undo" what your father did, but as long as you live in unforgiveness toward him, you will be held in horrible bondage. The alternative to not forgiving is simply not worth it. Begin by asking your heavenly Father to give you the strength to forgive and the freedom that comes from doing so.

THE BUZZ ON A BIBLE SHE

ANONYMOUS WOMAN

HER JAIL CELL: She had been trapped by an evil spirit for 18 years. She was all hunched over and couldn't stand up straight.

THEIR "CHANCE" ENCOUNTER: One Sabbath day Jesus was teaching in a Jewish temple, and he saw Ms. Anonymous. Without hesitation he called her over and said, "Dear woman, you are healed of your sickness!"

GETTING BAILED OUT: He touched her, and instantly she was free. She could stand up straight! Her response to her newfound freedom? She praised and thanked God.

THE WHINERS: The Temple bigwigs had just watched a miracle with their own eyes. But instead of falling to their knees in worship or telling everyone and their cousin about this guy, they complained that Jesus was healing on the Sabbath.

THE WINNERS: But Jesus' truth prevailed. "Isn't it right that she be released, even on the Sabbath?" So the woman was healed, and the people rejoiced at the wonderful things Jesus did.

WANT MORE DETAILS? For the whole scoop, check out Luke 13:10-17.

REBECCA SAYS

I met Anna during a songwriting session at a record label where she worked. When Anna offered to help, I was immediately drawn to her joyful spirit. Over lunch one day soon after we'd met, we began to connect because of our relationship with God. She later shared with me that she had been the victim of sexual abuse at the hand of her cousin. But instead of perpetuating this bondage, Anna broke free. She exuded such an infectious joy that I never would have guessed she had dealt with such tragedies in her life. I have watched her give her pain to God and work through her past with the help of wise believers, and as she does, her freedom continues to grow. Anna's life reminds me that freedom is possible, no matter what blows life has dealt you.

GiRL TALK!

WORRY FREE

Sit down with a couple of your friends and some lattes or chocolate cake. Write down the things you tend to worry about. Decide which category each falls under.

THINGS IN MY CONTROL
Write down action steps you can take to change this situation.

THINGS OUT OF MY CONTROL
Commit to giving this worry to God every day. Record each date you pray about it here.

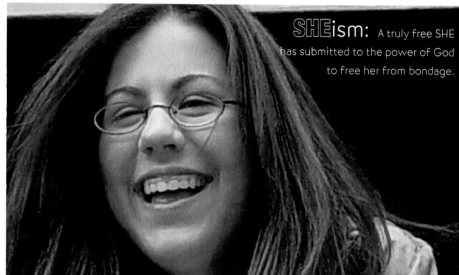

SHEism: A truly free SHE has submitted to the power of God to free her from bondage.

STAYING FREE

If you have gotten rid of both the Faker and Grudge Maker, you're well on your way to emotional freedom. You are free to be yourself AND free to forgive other people AND free to forgive yourself. But being free isn't a one-shot deal. Lurking around every corner, other Fakers, Grudge Makers, and their buddies are waiting to capture you again. Freedom is something you'll have to intentionally fight for until the day we're truly and completely free—the day we see Christ face-to-face. "All that I know now is partial and incomplete, but then I will know everything completely, just as God now knows me completely" (1 Corinthians 13:12).

SHE IS GUIDED

YOU DON'T HAVE TO WALK YOUR JOURNEY SOLO. GOD EMPOWERS YOU BY GIVING YOU
FOOTPRINTS TO FOLLOW.

The heartfelt counsel of a friend is as
sweet as perfume and incense.
Proverbs 27:9

Here is a poem I wrote, dedicated to a wonderful SHE who has been a huge blessing in my life . . . my mentor, Evie:

A LEGACY OF LOVE

REBECCA ST. JAMES

You have walked with me
My mentor friend,
You have lent me your listening ear
You have shared with me, you have understood
You have laughed with me through the years.

You who have lived before me,
Who have felt my pain, my fears,
I have cried upon your shoulder
Knowing that you, too, cried these tears.

You who sometimes learned the hard way
Your stories you have shared
Then I following along behind you,
From wayward paths have been spared.

The years have flown,
I'm a mentor now
Passing on your pearls from above
I praise God for you, my mentor friend
For you have left . . .
A legacy of love.

ANNOUNCING THE BIRTH OF . . . MENTOR!

The Greeks take credit for naming this whole mentoring idea, going way back to the stuff of myths. Did you ever think that the boring stuff you learned in English class would come in handy? Well, get this: When the Greek warrior Odysseus went off to fight in the Trojan War, he left his young son, Telemachus, in the care of a trusted guardian named Mentor. The war lasted 10 years, and it took another 10 years for Odysseus to get home. When he did, he found his son had grown into a fine man under the guidance of Mentor.

REBECCA SAYS

Growing up in Australia, I recall that my parents' record collection included a few albums by a smiling, petite blonde named Evie. I didn't know that 20 years later, God would use this little lady to make a profound impact on my life.

My parents had become acquainted with Evie when she had toured in Australia. Because of that connection, she and her husband, Pelle, came to our shows whenever we were in Florida close to where they live. Each time I saw Evie, she would encourage me both personally and in my ministry. Our personalities, our love for God, and our zest for life connected us. This bond was accentuated by the fact that she had walked where I was walking as a woman in the spotlight of Christian music. She understood me.

Over a period of time, I had become increasingly aware of my need for a mentor. I'd watched countless Christian artists lose their passion for ministry and become jaded, hurt, and hardened by what they had experienced due to physical, emotional, and spiritual demands to meet schedules and expectations. I wanted to stay soft before God and as a woman. I didn't want what I do as a profession to cripple me as a person.

After one visit with Evie, I felt a particular desire to ask her to mentor me. I prayed about the idea over the months to come, but I hesitated in asking her, not knowing what her response would be. Finally, one weekend early the next year, I sent Evie an e-mail expressing my desire. The following day, she called to say that she "just happened" to be visiting Nashville where I live (which I now know to be a rare occasion), and she asked if we could get together that night. I was excited to see God so obviously confirm that this mentoring relationship was right.

In her Opryland hotel room, Evie and I talked, shared, and began what is now one of the most treasured relationships of my life. I had found my mentor.

FAQs FREQUENTLY ASKED QUESTIONS

WHAT IS EMPOWERMENT?

Empowerment: the *E* in SHE

Empowerment: HimPowerment (the power we have through God)

WHAT'S THE BIG *E*?

Are you confused about what *empowerment* means? Yeah, we know you hear the word a lot, but it seems like it gets tossed around to mean everything from the stuff that keeps your car running to the stuff that motivates women's lib. So we wanna know . . .

- Do you want to have what it takes to meet any challenge that lies ahead for you?
- Do you want to meet life with enthusiasm and confidence?
- Do you want to live more than a mediocre life?
- Are you willing to stop leaning on yourself and your friends and your reputation, and start leaning on God as your source of strength?

If so, you are on your way to becoming the empowered woman God wants you to be. Remember, true empowerment happens only when you allow yourself to become Him-powered.

HOW DO I SIGN UP?

Sometimes God empowers us directly, through the Holy Spirit.

> You will receive power when the Holy Spirit comes upon you.
> Acts 1:8

Sometimes God empowers us through godly mentors, who teach us things they've already learned.

> You have heard me teach things that have been confirmed by many reliable witnesses. Now teach these truths to other trustworthy people who will be able to pass them on to others.
> 2 Timothy 2:2

YEAH, BUT . . .

- I can handle life on my own.
- I feel unworthy of having someone else invest in my life.
- I feel abandoned by people I've looked up to.
- I feel awkward asking for help.
- The adults around me don't seem to have the answers anyway.
- I feel as if I have too much on my plate and too many mistakes of my own to be telling others how to live.
- I don't have enough experience to help anyone else.

WE GET SPAMMED FROM ALL DIRECTIONS WITH LIES THAT LIFE IS ALL ABOUT *ME*.

"BECAUSE I'M WORTH IT" (L'OREAL)

"HAVE IT YOUR WAY" (BURGER KING)

"LIVE LIFE IN YOUR OWN LANE" (MERCURY)

"AN ARMY OF ONE" (U.S. ARMY)

"YOU DESERVE A BREAK TODAY" (McDONALD'S)

REBECCA SAYS

The apostle Paul taught Timothy, who taught other faithful believers, who taught others. Someone taught Evie. Evie teaches me what she has learned. I teach others what I have learned, and they teach others what they've learned. That's the godly mentoring model.

FAQs FREQUENTLY ASKED QUESTIONS

WHAT IS MENTORING?

Mentoring: a friendship that involves one woman helping another woman become the person God designed her to be

WHAT MAKES A GOOD MENTOR?

Mentor: someone who offers insights about life and faith

Mentor: someone who leads the mentee in a growing relationship with God and helps her become empowered to mentor someone else
Mentor: YOU!

WHAT MAKES A GOOD MENTEE?

Mentee: someone who is teachable and ready to grow
Mentee: YOU!

Obey your spiritual leaders, and do what they say. Their work is to watch over your souls, and they are accountable to God.
Hebrews 13:17

MENTORS:
SHED YOUR CAMO!

Can you ID the role of a mentor? In each of the following pairs, decide which action a true mentor should take.

- [ ] **a.** Assist you
- [ ] **b.** Fix you

- [ ] **a.** Tell you
- [ ] **b.** Guide you

- [ ] **a.** Lord it over you
- [ ] **b.** Walk alongside you

- [ ] **a.** Look backward with you
- [ ] **b.** Look forward with you

- [ ] **a.** Help you grow from past hurts
- [ ] **b.** Rehash the hurts with you

- [ ] **a.** Encourage you to depend on your mentor
- [ ] **b.** Encourage you to depend on God

- [ ] **a.** Capitalize on your God-given strengths
- [ ] **b.** Focus on your weaknesses

DID YOU SPOT THE MENTOR?
(The best mentors would do this: a, b, b, b, a, b, a.)

GiRL TALK!

Along with a couple of friends, brainstorm these two lists.

QUALITIES YOU WOULD LIKE IN A MENTOR:

WOMEN YOU THINK WOULD MAKE GOOD MENTORS:

QUALITIES YOU WOULD LIKE TO PROVIDE AS A MENTOR FOR SOMEONE ELSE:

ONE PERSON YOU MIGHT LIKE TO MENTOR: (Think of a younger girl who is in a similar situation as you've been in or who is struggling in an area you've already worked through.)

Don't let anyone think less of you because you are young.
1 Timothy 4:12

SPEAKS

JENNIFER (18)

She's three years older and the one who guides me spiritually. When I have tough decisions to make, I go to her. We don't agree about everything, but we rarely argue. Instead we talk it out, and she tells me why she thinks something would be wrong for me based on her experiences. When we do argue, we always apologize to each other within a few hours. She has shaped and influenced me a lot. I'm glad I have her in my life.

SPEAKS

SAMANTHA (19)

I met her last summer while working at a Young Life camp, and we bonded instantly. Over this past year, we've been talking on the phone every Friday and diving into the Word of God. She helps keep me accountable, and we are both very honest with each other. She is 10 years older than me. God's hand is totally in the relationship, controlling the way it goes.

THE LIE:
I'll never find a mentor.

THE TRUTH:
GOD HAS SOMEONE—OR SOME *ONES*—CUSTOM-MADE TO MENTOR YOU. BE ON THE LOOKOUT.

FOOTSTEPS TO FOLLOW

WHAT DO YOU WANT TO GAIN FROM YOUR MENTORING RELATIONSHIP?

- Prayer support
- Wisdom
- Encouragement
- Accountability
- A sounding board
- Biblical truth
- Experience
- A different perspective
- Connection to others
- Vision for the bigger picture
- Other:_____

WHAT'S MY FIRST STEP?

Pray for a mentor.

WHAT SHOULD MY MENTOR LOOK LIKE?

She should:

- be a woman of deep integrity
- be respected by and consulted by other Christians
- demonstrate a mature and consistent lifestyle
- be willing to sacrifice time and energy and be willing to commit for the long haul
- keep the content of your times together confidential
- demonstrate wisdom, patience, and emotional and spiritual maturity
- cultivate relationships
- offer a network of resources
- talk as well as listen
- show concern with your interests[1]

WHERE SHOULD I DO MY MENTOR SHOPPING?

- Look over your list of wants and needs in a mentor.
- Go to your church leaders or youth group leader and ask for recommendations and referrals.
- Think of women you admire and want to be like.

- Call a woman you've watched and admired. Ask to meet with her about a specific issue. Use a go-between to set up a meeting if it feels more comfortable.
- Don't mention the word *mentor* until you see if that's where God takes you.
- Get to know her better to see if God might be leading you to this particular woman.
- Ask for her advice about a specific challenge you're facing or for clarity on a Scripture you've read.
- Ask about her mentors and other women she has helped.

SPEAKS

AALIYAH (18)

My grandma and I have a special relationship. Before my grandfather died, I was privileged to lead him to the Lord. Then my grandma also became a believer. This past year I have gone to visit her once or twice a week, and we just talk for several hours on end. We talk about our struggles and our schedules, and we even go shopping or out to eat together. I have come to enjoy doing work for her and occasionally running errands for her.

SHE ASKS

ELINA (15)

Does my mentor have to be a woman? I consider my youth group leader my biggest mentor. He is there any time—day or night—that I need him. And what do you think about my boyfriend being my mentor? He is the person most like me, and I trust him the most. He brings out the best in me. He makes me confident in myself and gives me a feeling of self-worth.

REBECCA SAYS

There is definitely a place for having male leaders in your life whom you can respect and look up to—especially if your own dad isn't in the picture very much. But I believe that as a girl your mentor needs to be an older woman. Since the age of 15, I have worked in an industry with many older guys—in my band, in the studio, and at my record label. Because of my desire to live a life that is pure and above reproach, I've had to be very careful and wise in the way I work with men. I try to avoid allowing any unhealthy attachments to take place from spending too much time with a guy or by seeing him as a mentor, knowing that either situation could lead to trouble. I also don't think it's wise to have your boyfriend as your mentor. There are certain thoughts, emotions, and "times of the month" that only other females can relate to. Women make the best mentors for us girls!

> *Older women must train the younger women . . . to live wisely and be pure.*
> Titus 2:4-5

THE LIE: No one would want me to be her mentor.

THE TRUTH: SOMEONE DESPERATELY NEEDS YOU TO HELP HER DO LIFE.

SHE ASKS

JASMINE (14)

I feel like my mentor is myself. I can be who I want to be as long as it doesn't go against God's laws. Is it okay to think of myself as my own mentor?

REBECCA SAYS

Have you ever heard the expression "No man is an island"? God did not make us to live without the input of others. Picture yourself as an island. What happens when the storms come and a "ship" wrecks on your island? What do you do? Who do you turn to? We need godly people outside ourselves to help us know how to live.

SHE'S BEEN THERE

Get together with a godly woman, and pray with her about finding a mentor. Have her help you find addresses of women you admire in your community, your church, or even on the national level. Meet with this woman in person, give her a call, or e-mail her (see sample note below). Get to know her. Ask her questions about the lessons she has learned and how God has worked in her life.

Dear _____,

I find myself at an important stage of life right now. I want to be ready for the challenges and opportunities that lie ahead. Because your example has meant so much to me, I want to ask you a favor. Would you take a few minutes to write me or e-mail me about an important lesson or truth you think I should know? I respect your insights, and I'm grateful for your influence in my life.

Thanks,

FOOTSTEPS I LEAVE BEHIND

HOW DO I START?
Pray for someone to mentor.

WHERE SHOULD I DO MY MENTEE SHOPPING?
- Brainstorm two or three girls in your life you could come alongside as a friend to help them become the women God designed them to be.
- Go to your church leaders or youth pastor and ask for recommendations and referrals.
- Keep your eyes open for someone who needs what you can provide.
- Call or write a letter to one girl you're thinking about mentoring. Ask to meet with her.
- Don't mention the word *mentor* until you see if that's where God takes you.
- Get to know her better to see if God might be leading you to her.
- Ask her about a specific challenge she's facing. Pray silently for godly advice you might provide.
- Arrange your next meeting.

WHAT DO I HAVE TO GIVE?
- Experiences I can talk about with the girl I mentor:

....

....

- Interests we share:

....

....

- Qualities I possess that I can use in my mentoring (listening, compassion, wisdom):

....

....

Here's how to pick out at least one other person who could use a good dose of your guidance.

Dear _____,

Before you know it, you'll be my age. I know God has great plans for you, and I'm glad I am able to be part of your life. As someone just a few steps ahead of you, I wanted to share an important lesson I've learned along the way. I hope it'll help you too.

[Tell a story from your life and what you learned from the experience.]

I'm here if you ever need me.

_____

OKAY, NOW WHAT?

So now you have a mentor and a girl to mentor. What do you do next? There's no magic formula, but here are some tips to get you started. Just pick out whatever works for the two of you.

CHOOSE YOUR HAUNT

A coffee shop

A bookstore

Your favorite lunch café

Your house

Her house

Somewhere that's comfortable and where you can have meaningful conversations

INK IT

Schedule your meetings and stick to 'em.

Each mentoring relationship is different, but once a month might be a good place to start.

Decide ahead of time how long you're going to meet (an hour? two?).

SKETCH OUT A GAME PLAN

Pray.

Talk about life, faith, relationships, and decisions.

Choose a book of the Bible to study.

Read and talk about a book you're both interested in.

COOKIE-CUTTER MENTORING?

Oh, and one more thing. Not all mentoring relationships are the same.

Some are formal. Others are pretty laid back.

Some are short-term. Others last for decades.

Some involve a mentor who is much older than the mentee. Others involve two people who are pretty close to the same age.

Some address a specific need. Others cover a variety of different life experiences.

You just need to decide what's the best fit for the two of you.

REBECCA SAYS

One summer afternoon some time ago, I was standing beside the small storage barn in my backyard, pouring out my heart to my mentor, Evie, who was on the other end of the phone line. She listened with a great deal of understanding as I shared with her my fears that I'd once again face burnout and that I would someday hit the wall and be crippled by the crash. I'll never forget what she told me that day. She said, "Rebecca, just you being aware of this weakness will help you guard against it ever happening and will help bring victory over it."

Months later, a younger female friend for whom I've become an informal mentor shared her heart with me. She told of insecurities in her life that she feared would turn into actions and then into hardness of heart. I began to share with her, "My friend, just you being aware of this weakness will help you . . ."

I discovered afresh the joy and beauty of having—and being—a mentor.

TOP 5 MENTOR ?s

(questions you can ask your mentor)

1. What is something you wish you'd known when you were my age?

2. What is one of your favorite passages of Scripture?

3. What is something you've learned about God lately?

4. What is one book that has affected your life?

5. What are some areas in my life that I could grow in?

TOP 5 MENTEE ?s

(questions you can ask the girl you mentor)

1. What is something you are struggling with right now?

2. What are some of your dreams and goals?

3. How have you seen God work this week?

4. What have you read in the Bible lately that has been convicting you?

5. How can I be praying for you?

As iron sharpens iron, so a friend sharpens a friend.
Proverbs 27:17

THE BUZZ ON TWO BIBLE SHES

NAOMI AND RUTH

THEIR CLAIM TO FAME:	Ruth is one of only five women named in Jesus' lineup of ancestors. Plus, her love story with Boaz is one of the first recorded in history. And all this happened thanks to her relationship with her mentor, Naomi.
ENTER TROUBLE:	Years earlier, Naomi and her husband had moved from Bethlehem to the evil country of Moab to escape a famine. Their sons had married women there, Ruth and Orpah. Later all three of these women—Naomi, Ruth, and Orpah—lost their husbands, and they were faced with the question of what to do next.
HUSBAND SHOPPING OR BACK TO BETHLEHEM?	Orpah remained in Moab where the husband-hunting odds were greatest. But Ruth insisted on staying with and learning from Naomi. Together they headed back to Bethlehem. Ruth went to work, gathering grain in the fields of Boaz, a distant relative of Naomi's husband. That's when God used Naomi and Ruth's mentoring friendship to accomplish his incredible plans.
CHECK OUT WHAT HAPPENED:	Ruth married Boaz. Ruth and Boaz had a son named Obed. Obed became the grandfather of David. David was born into the direct line of Jesus Christ.
ANOTHER HAPPY SHE-LIFE ENDING:	The same Providence who directed Ruth to the right Bethlehem field later led the magi to that same town to see the Savior. A mile east of Bethlehem stands that "Field of Boaz"—the spot where Ruth picked grain. The field next to it is called the "Field of the Shepherds." Tradition holds that the angels first proclaimed Christ's birth over that spot. In the place where Ruth and Boaz met, over a thousand years later angels sang, "Glory to God in highest heaven, and peace on earth to those with whom God is pleased" (Luke 2:14).
ANATOMY OF A MENTOR:	Naomi walked alongside Ruth. Naomi suffered with her and rejoiced with her. Naomi gave Ruth godly advice. Naomi pointed her to God's desire for her life. And God used the friendship of women to accomplish his plan.
WANT MORE DETAILS?	For the whole scoop, check out Ruth 1–4.

YOU

the world
(over 2 billion kids)
——————▷

What can you possibly do?

Help ONE.

Visit www.compassion.com
and see what you really can do.

(800) 336-7676
www.compassion.com

Releasing children from poverty
Compassion
in Jesus' name

SHEism: A TRULY MENTORED SHE IS A GIRL WHO USES MENTORING
TO MAKE HER OWN LIFE AND THE LIVES OF OTHERS BETTER.

The boundary lines have fallen for me in pleasant places.
Psalm 16:6, NIV

SHE IS BOUNDARIED

GOD EMPOWERS YOU AND BALANCES YOU THROUGH BOUNDARIES.

Kayla allows PMS to affect her emotional responses.

Amy has trouble saying no, so she constantly overcommits.

Beth is confused by the spiritual philosophies she reads and hears at school.

Dana goes from one bad relationship to another.

Kristin's spending is out of control.

Heidi's room is so messy she can't seem to find anything she needs.

WHAT DO THESE GIRLS HAVE IN COMMON?

a) They're not in control of at least one area of their life.

b) They are in need of clear boundaries in at least one area of their life.

c) Both a and b

d) None of the above

If you chose C, give yourself a pat on the back, but look out—we're about to take a look at *your* boundaries too.

I, the LORD, define the ocean's sandy shoreline as an everlasting boundary that the waters cannot cross. The waves may toss and roar, but they can never pass the boundaries I set.
Jeremiah 5:22

QUIZ: DRAWING THE LINE

Do you draw your boundaries with permanent marker? pencil? nothing at all?

DO YOU . . .

1. Run from one activity or commitment to another?

   yes   no

2. Get overemotional when coping with expectations placed on you at school or at home?

   yes   no

3. Have fuzzy guidelines about how far you'll go with a guy?

   yes   no

4. Find yourself constantly wasting time?

   yes   no

5. Spend more money than you have?

   yes   no

6. Have trouble recognizing signs of spiritual abuse and manipulation?

   yes   no

7. Feel more sensitive than you should at certain times of the month?

   yes   no

8. Struggle to balance how much to eat, exercise, and rest?

   yes   no

9. Find it difficult to feel content with what you have?

   yes   no

10. Choose unsafe friends?

    yes   no

11. Have a record of unhealthy relationships with guys?

    yes   no

12. Fail to spend personal time in prayer and Bible reading?

    yes   no

YOU MAY NEED SOME PERMANENT MARKER ACTION FOR . . .

your emotional boundaries if you answered *yes* to 2 or 7

your physical boundaries if you answered *yes* to 3 or 8

your spiritual boundaries if you answered *yes* to 6 or 12

your relational boundaries if you answered *yes* to 10 or 11

your financial boundaries if you answered *yes* to 5 or 9

your organizational boundaries if you answered *yes* to 1 or 4

You've inherited a life of boundary turf wars. Since Adam blamed Eve and Eve blamed the snake for their decision to eat from the forbidden tree (see Genesis 3:12-13), accepting responsibility and taking control of our own life has not come easily. We explain away our behavior with all kinds of excuses, and then we wonder why things get out of control. We have not set limits to guide us. We have failed to guard our emotional, physical, spiritual, relational, financial, and organizational turf.

[God] created all the nations throughout the whole earth. He decided beforehand when they should rise and fall, and he determined their boundaries.

Acts 17:26

REBECCA SAYS

The century "two thousand" we now live in might be renamed the "century *too* thousand." We are too busy, too overworked, too overcommitted, too well fed, too entertained, too stressed, and as a result, too unhappy. We are a culture without boundaries—not just in the areas of time and commitment, but in most other areas as well.

DID YA KNOW . . .

- Average hours of sleep teens need per night: 9.5
- Average hours of sleep teens get per night: 7.4[1]
- Forty-five percent of college students are in credit-card debt. Their average debt is $3,066.
- Twenty-eight percent of students with a credit card say they roll over credit-card debt each month.
- In recent years there has been more than a 50 percent increase in bankruptcies declared by people under 25.[2]
- An estimated 5 to 7 million Americans have been involved in cults or cultlike groups.
- About 180,000 people get sucked into cults every year.[3]

You are in charge of your own choices. One way God gives you empowerment—HimPowerment—is through boundaries. Boundaries don't confine you—they free you up.
Boundaries give you self-control.

YEAH, BUT . . .

- Boundaries are different for different people.
- None of my friends have boundaries.
- If I set boundaries, people won't like me.
- I'll hurt people's feelings when I say no.
- Other:_____

You set the boundaries of the earth, and you made both summer and winter.
Psalm 74:17

REBECCA SAYS

In a funny way, I learned about the importance of boundaries at an early age. When I was about eight years old, my family and I stayed at my grandparents' house during the holidays. Of my six siblings, my brother Daniel is closest to my age. Probably because we were the older, more responsible children, we got lumped into a bed together. I had a feeling that wasn't going to work out from the get-go, so I warned him, "Stay on your side!" He must have seen this as an invitation to annoy me, because soon afterward, a foot crept over to my side of the bed and touched me on the leg. I, the ever-patient-and-mature older sister, kicked it back. The war continued until a higher authority in the form of our mother entered the room and the blame game began. Soon enough, the boundary line was drawn by a rolled-up blanket down the middle of the bed! Just as I needed a physical boundary with my brother, so we all need boundaries in our life—emotionally, physically, spiritually, and relationally, just to name a few.

"That's an amazing thought—that God would use me, a regular Joe Schmoe, a teenager. . . . I might be young, but I want to be a good steward of what God has given me. Not just with music, because my voice could be gone someday. But I want to reflect God with my life."
Joy Williams[4]

WHAT ARE BOUNDARY TURF WARS?

Boundary turf wars: battles you fight to keep yourself safe and healthy

Boundary turf wars: combat between the world's ways and God's ways over the turf of your emotions, body, soul, relationships, money, time, and stuff

Boundary turf wars: wars that won't be completely won until we get to heaven, but that God helps us manage now

WHAT'S THE POINT OF FIGHTING BOUNDARY TURF WARS?

Boundaries bring you peace and security.

Boundaries give you confidence to move forward.

Boundaries create consistency for your decisions.

Boundaries bring balance.

Boundaries please God.

Better to have self-control than to conquer a city.
Proverbs 16:32

SHE GETS PERSONAL

Check the statements that best reflect your own boundary turf wars.

☐ I've never seen important adults in my life model effective boundaries.

☐ No one has told me how to draw boundaries in my life.

☐ I know the boundaries I should keep, but I don't know how to fight for them.

☐ The boundaries I've already tried haven't worked, so I've just about given up fighting for them.

☐ I have my boundaries set and usually stick to them, but sometimes I need help redefining them and sticking to them.

For God has not given us a spirit of fear and timidity, but of power, love, and self-discipline.
2 Timothy 1:7

EMOTIONAL TURF WARS

Do your feelings decide your behavior?	yes	no
Do you worry about the future?	yes	no
Does anger overtake your reason?	yes	no
Do you shut down emotionally when you're stressed out?	yes	no

If you answered *yes* to any of these questions, you may need to gear up for some emotional turf wars.

WHY SHOULD I CARE?

- Emotional boundaries show us how to handle our emotions. They keep in check how much we allow ourselves to be affected by others.
- Without emotional boundaries, we either ignore our emotions or allow them to control our responses. And we fail to keep a healthy distance from the uncontrolled, unreliable emotions of others.

TIPS FOR WINNING THIS TURF WAR

- Take charge of your feelings—don't let them make your decisions for you.
- Look your emotions in the eye—don't stuff them in your closet.
- Understand what triggers your emotional reactions, and learn how to deal with those situations in a healthy way.

SHE SPEAKS

BETHANY (16)

I got in a fight with my mom again the other day just before my period. I wish I could learn to keep my mouth shut for a couple of days to see if I still feel as strongly about the issues. Maybe I wouldn't get in as many fights.

SHE GETS PERSONAL

Think of a time recently when your emotions controlled you and remember the damage it did. How do anger, worry, and stress affect your behavior?

....

....

....

....

Getting wisdom is the wisest thing you can do! And whatever else you do, develop good judgment.
Proverbs 4:7

PHYSICAL TURF WARS

Put a mark next to the phrases that describe the typical you.

- ☐ lazy; sleep too much
- ☐ eat too much
- ☐ exercise too often

- ☐ overstretched; don't sleep enough
- ☐ don't eat enough
- ☐ don't work out enough

If your balance is off, it may be time for some physical turf battles!

JESSICA (17)

Usually when I wake up in the morning, the first thing I think about is what I'm going to eat. I invariably go to bed that night with guilt over what I did eat.

WHY SHOULD I CARE?

- Physical boundaries help us take care of our body.
- Without physical boundaries, we neglect the things that are good for us and allow harmful habits to form instead.

TIPS FOR WINNING THIS TURF WAR

- Set specific goals for taking care of your body.
- Get a friend on board to keep you accountable. (Maybe she can be your workout buddy or the friend who orders a salad instead of fries with you at McDonald's.)

Think clearly and exercise self-control.
1 Peter 1:13

SPIRITUAL TURF WARS

Put a mark next to the phrases that describe the typical you.

- ☐ reject any beliefs that seem unpopular at school
- ☐ no Christian friends or accountability
- ☐ spiritually burned out (lots of service, little recharging)
- ☐ don't trust my spiritual leaders

- ☐ blindly accept whatever I'm taught
- ☐ no interaction with unbelievers; live in the Christian ghetto
- ☐ spiritually fat (lots of input, little outreach)
- ☐ depend completely on leaders for spiritual knowledge

If your marks lean toward one side or the other, it may be time to start defending your spiritual turf.

WHY SHOULD I CARE?

- Spiritual boundaries start when we decide to follow Christ. They continue as we grow in our faith and seek to please God with our decisions.
- Without spiritual boundaries we won't be able to recognize lies, and we won't have nonnegotiable truths to build our life on.

TIPS FOR WINNING THIS TURF WAR

- Read your Bible every day in your favorite place. God will talk to you there.
- Whenever you're facing a challenge (such as whether or not to talk about someone else behind her back or whether or not to let a friend off the hook for hurting you), go back to the Bible and find out what God has to say about it.
- Pray every day. Check out this verse: "Look! I stand at the door and knock. If you hear my voice and open the door, I will come in, and we will share a meal together as friends" (Revelation 3:20). That means God wants you to do breakfast—or lunch or dinner—with him. He wants to tell you what's on his heart and for you to tell him what's on yours.
- Pray the ACTS prayer—when you're walking, showering, or lying in your bed.

Adoration (praise God for who he is)

Confession (ask him to forgive you for a sin)

Thanksgiving (express gratitude for what he has already done for you)

Supplication (bring your needs before him)

SHE SPEAKS

SIERRA (17)

I'm leaving for college this fall, and I still don't know what I believe even though I've been in church all my life. Spiritually I could be in trouble.

SHE GETS PERSONAL

Describe a time recently when something confused you spiritually.

....

....

....

....

....

....

Think of things your parents believe in that you're not sure about yourself.

....

....

....

....

....

Talk to your parents or an adult mentor about these things.

RELATIONAL TURF WARS

Do you find that people often take advantage of you
at school or at work?   yes   no
Do you find yourself getting close to unsafe people?   yes   no
Do you find yourself in codependent relationships
(where someone controls or manipulates you)?   yes   no

If you answered *yes* to any of these questions, it's time to stake out your relational turf.

WHY SHOULD I CARE?

- Relational boundaries set guidelines for what we will and will not accept from others. They help us develop healthy, lasting relationships.
- Without relational boundaries, dangerous people can hurt or take advantage of us.

TIPS FOR WINNING THIS TURF WAR

- Get an inner circle of healthy relationships—friends who love you and love God and help you grow.
- Recognize that some people (the ones who suck the life out of you) should just stay at the acquaintance level. And that's okay.
- Learn the difference between being a servant and being stepped on.

SHE ASKS
CHELSEA (18)
I keep dating sicko guys. What's wrong with me?

REBECCA SAYS

There's nothing wrong with *you*—you just need to work on your relational boundaries. It's important to know a lot about the character of a guy before you date/court him. Once you have a sense that a guy may be starting to emotionally or physically abuse you in any way, get out! You need to respect yourself enough to know that you don't need this in your life. Also, keep in mind that a healthy self-image does not come from having a boyfriend. Be picky—don't settle for anything less than a God-honoring guy who also honors you.

SHE GETS PERSONAL

Describe some unhealthy decisions you've made because your friends were a bad influence.

....

....

....

....

Think of a relationship in your life that could be healthier. What went wrong?

....

....

....

....

FINANCIAL TURF WARS

Are you in credit-card debt?	yes	no
Do you go "therapy shopping" (spending money to try to make yourself feel better)?	yes	no
Do you find yourself wishing you had what's-her-name's clothes, music, purse, shoes . . . ?	yes	no

WHY SHOULD I CARE?

- Financial boundaries set lifetime standards for how you will and will not spend money.
- Without financial boundaries, your money will be gone—and so will your peace—before you spend it on things that truly matter.

TIPS FOR WINNING THIS TURF WAR

- Decide what's important to you. Where your cash flows, there your heart goes (Matthew 6:21).
- Pay the important stuff first—God deserves better than your leftovers.

SHE SPEAKS

HAYLEIGH (17)
I keep overcharging my credit card. I can't seem to stop.

SHE GETS PERSONAL

Take out your most recent credit-card statement or your check registry (or pull out your receipts from the past month). Make a list of the things you bought.

....

....

....

Think of the last time you felt guilty over how much money you spent.

....

....

....

What's something you don't spend *enough* money on?

....

....

....

[God] created the horizon when he separated the waters; he set the boundary between day and night.
Job 26:10

ORGANIZATIONAL TURF WARS

What do these things look like right now?

	Total trash heap	I can find most of the stuff I'm looking for	Mr. Clean would be proud
my bedroom			
my locker			
my book bag			
my purse			
my car			

WHY SHOULD I CARE?

- Organizational boundaries bring order to chaos.
- Without organizational boundaries, clutter results—too many commitments, a frantic mind, and unclear goals.

TIPS FOR WINNING THIS TURF WAR

- Your stuff: Know when to give away, put away, throw away.
- Your time: Know when to say no.
- Your internal world: Know when to be still before God.

SHE SPEAKS

EMILY (20)

I always thought I just had to live as a messy person. Then it dawned on me . . . that's a pet sin, and I don't want to be stuck in that. I want to fix these habits now so they don't follow me into adulthood.

SHE GETS PERSONAL

Where is your life most disorganized?

....

....

....

Have you noticed a pattern of when chaos tends to creep in?

....

....

....

Be still, and know that I am God!
Psalm 46:10

GIRL! TALK!

Grab a couple of friends who love you and who will be totally honest with you.

What boundary turf wars are you struggling with?

- Emotional
- Physical
- Spiritual
- Relational
- Financial
- Organizational

Start tackling one of those turfs right now. Not sure where to start? Here are a few ideas:

- Write in your journal to process some of the up-and-down emotions you've faced this week.
- Go to the gym.
- Read a chapter of Proverbs and talk about it with a friend.
- Call up a friend with whom you have an unhealthy relationship and talk about one thing you can change in your friendship.
- Make a plan for spending next month's money.
- Clean your room.

SHE'S BEEN THERE

Go out to eat with your mom, your mentor, or another godly woman. Ask her what boundaries are most valuable to her in each of these areas—and if there were boundaries she wishes she'd had when she was your age.

- Emotional
- Physical
- Spiritual
- Relational
- Financial
- Organizational

SHE ASKS

JOANNA (18)

My mom had me when she was really young, and she has never seemed too sure of herself when it comes to being a mom. She has never told me anything about boundaries, and her life shows everything BUT boundaries. I recently became a Christian after attending youth group with a friend. I guess what I'm asking is, is it ever too late to start building boundaries, or do you need to start when you're young?

REBECCA SAYS

When I was a little girl, from time to time I would pull everything out of my closet—keepsakes, clothes, shoes . . . everything. What a mess! Then I would reorganize, throw away what I no longer needed, and carefully put back what I still valued and wanted. Just like this little routine I held as a child, I think it's important for us to pull out the "clutter" from the closet of our life and reorganize our boundaries. Sometimes things need to be thrown away—things like bad habits and unimportant time-wasters. It's easy to close the closet doors and ignore the chaotic, disorganized areas of our life, hoping they'll just go away. But God wants us to bring out into the open those areas that need changing. Is it ever too late to allow God to bring order from chaos? Absolutely not!

THE BUZZ ON A BIBLE SHE

WISDOM

THE DISCLAIMER:	Just so you know . . . this Bible SHE is different from the others in the book. For one thing, well, technically she's not a living, breathing woman like the others. Confused? Let us explain. In Proverbs, the author describes the concept of wisdom by giving it human traits (your English teacher would call it personification, but we won't get into that). So we're going to talk about Wisdom like she's a woman here, but don't take it too far, okay? Know that God is the source of wisdom, and any wisdom we have comes from him.

THE FIRST SHE:	*The LORD formed me from the beginning, before he created anything else. I was appointed in ages past, at the very first, before the earth began. I was born before the oceans were created, before the springs bubbled forth their waters. Before the mountains were formed, before the hills, I was born—before he had made the earth and fields and the first handfuls of soil.* Wisdom has been with God waaaay back, since the beginning. And all the smart decisions that people have made from then until now have the fingerprints of Wisdom on them. *I, Wisdom, live together with good judgment.*

SINCE WHEN?	Wisdom has seen fashions go in and out of style more times than Jessica Simpson can change her shoes (at a recent glance into her e-closet, it looks like Jess has at least 139 pairs.)[5] *I was there when he established the heavens, when he drew the horizon on the oceans.* *I was there when he set the clouds above, when he established springs deep in the earth.* *I was there when he set the limits of the seas, so they would not spread beyond their boundaries . . . when he marked off the earth's foundations.*

WISDOM'S RÉSUMÉ:	*I was the architect at [God's] side. I was his constant delight, rejoicing always in his presence.*

WHY YOU WANT WISDOM TO SIT AT YOUR LUNCH TABLE:	Wisdom was there when God created the boundaries of the earth, and now she is ready to help *you* draw the boundaries for your life. *And so, my children, listen to me, for all who follow my ways are joyful. Listen to my instruction and be wise. Don't ignore it. Joyful are those who listen to me.* Wisdom will help you fight all your turf wars. *For whoever finds me finds life and receives favor from the LORD.*

WANT MORE DETAILS?	Surprised by what you see? Check out Proverbs 8:1-36.

Don't turn your back on wisdom, for she will protect you. Love her, and she will guard you. . . . If you prize wisdom, she will make you great. Embrace her, and she will honor you.

Proverbs 4:6, 8

SHEism: The truly boundaried SHE is a girl who asks herself *Is it wise?* and who maintains strong, biblical boundaries.

"I know the plans I have for you," says the Lᴏʀᴅ. *"They are plans for good and not for disaster, to give you a future and a hope."*

Jeremiah 29:11

SHE IS PURPOSEFUL

GOD EMPOWERS YOU BY GIVING YOU A PURPOSE TO FULFILL.

FAQs FREQUENTLY ASKED QUESTIONS

WHAT IS PURPOSE?

Purpose gives us focus to know what's important.

Purpose gives us direction to know where to go.

Purpose gives us strength to do what we need to do.

SHE GETS PERSONAL

Do you feel confused about your purpose in life? Why or why not?

....

....

....

....

Do you have a God-given vision for the future? What is it?

....

....

....

....

Do you feel that you are on a mission daily?

....

....

....

....

THINK ABOUT IT . . .

Everything you do to fulfill your purpose will matter for eternity. What have you done recently for eternity's sake?

WHAT'S THE POINT OF LIFE?
People have tried to figure out the answer to this question forever—celebrities, writers, scientists, regular people. How can we know? The famous author Franz Kafka figured there wasn't much to live for, saying that "the meaning of life is that it stops."[1] If you're looking for a more contemporary answer, you could try *The Simpsons*—after all, Dr. Kris Jozajtis (a college prof in Scotland) thinks that "the Simpsons are in many ways a source of moral orientation, even on the big issues such as the meaning of life."[2] No offense to the Simpsons, but doesn't it seem like there's got to be more to life?

Here's where some celebs say they find meaning or purpose in life.[3]

"We have similar ultimate goals in life. Right now, it's to finish high school, go to college in the fall, and stay in business."
MARY-KATE AND ASHLEY OLSEN

"Reality is wrong. Dreams are for real."
TUPAC SHAKUR

"The meaning of life is . . . to move ahead, to go up, to achieve, to conquer."
ARNOLD SCHWARZENEGGER

"When I walked into class and heard them talking about art and acting and about becoming greater than you are, it was like music to my ears. I thought, *This is it. I have my purpose in life*."
MARK RUFFALO

"What is life? / Life is like a big obstacle / put in front of your optical to slow you down / and everytime you think you gotten past it / it's gonna come back around and tackle you to the d--- ground."
FROM "IF I HAD. . ." BY EMINEM

"I don't have a regular life, but what is a regular life, anyway? Whatever happens in life is fine. Just trust in that."
ORLANDO BLOOM

"Open wide and swallow their meaning of life / I can't make it work your way / Thanks but no thanks."
FROM "MEANING OF LIFE" BY THE OFFSPRING

Kinda depressing, huh? If these famous people are right and life is all about acting, getting ahead, and just letting whatever happens happen (or if there *is* no purpose in life, as some of them seem to be saying), then what's the point?

But for us as Christ-followers, that's not all there is. God doesn't leave us in the dark about what we're here on earth for. He created you for a purpose, and he has a plan for your life. And not just any old plan. A good plan. A designed-just-for-you plan. Wanna find it?

TOP 10 **MEANINGS OF LIFE**
ACADEMIC ACCORDING TO FAMOUS PEOPLE[4]

1. "To enjoy or experience life." Helen Keller, Eleanor Roosevelt, Janis Joplin, and Cary Grant all thought so.

2. "To love, help, or serve others." This gave purpose to Albert Einstein, Jean-Jacques Rousseau, and the Dalai Lama.

3. "Life is a mystery," according to Bob Dylan, Napoleon Bonaparte, and Stephen Hawking.

4. "Life is meaningless." If you take this pessimistic viewpoint, you share it with Sigmund Freud, Franz Kafka, and Jean-Paul Sartre.

5. "Life is a struggle," at least for Charles Dickens, Jonathan Swift, and Benjamin Disraeli.

6. "To contribute to something that is greater than ourselves." Benjamin Franklin, Richard Nixon, and Ralph Waldo Emerson all subscribed to this opinion.

7. "To become self-actualized"—whatever that means, which was evidently something to Marie Curie, Plato, and Robert Louis Stevenson.

8. "To create your own meaning." Carl Sagan, Simone de Beauvoir, and Carl Jung placed bets on this one.

9. "Life is absurd or a joke." Is it any surprise to hear that this is the opinion of Charlie Chaplin? Oscar Wilde and Albert Camus agreed with him.

10. "To serve or worship God and prepare for the next (or after-) life." You guessed it . . . Billy Graham, Mother Teresa, and Martin Luther King Jr. all sided with this meaning of life.

REBECCA SAYS

When I was 12 years old, I attended a service at my Christian school that significantly impacted my life story. A speaker asked people to come forward if they felt God leading them to give their gifts and talents to him. I felt led by God to respond and ask for his direction in discovering his will and purpose for my life. It was that same year that God began to lead me into music.

One of life's greatest tragedies is not death, but life without discovering your individual God-given purpose. You don't really live unless you know why you're alive.

YEAH, BUT . . .

- My life is too ordinary to have any real purpose.

- I can worry about my life purpose when I'm older.

- I'm just one person—I can't make that big of a difference.

- Isn't the purpose of life just to be happy?

- I've messed up God's purpose for my life.

- Other:_____

PURPOSELESS or PURPOSEFULL?

Remember *Alice in Wonderland*? In the story by Lewis Carroll that inspired the movie, Alice comes to a fork in the road. She asks the Cheshire Cat which direction she should take.

"That depends a good deal on where you want to get to," said the Cat.
"I don't much care where," said Alice.
"Then it doesn't matter which way you walk," said the Cat.

You face similar choices and forks in the road each day. If you don't care where you are headed, then you (and Alice!) will probably find yourself lost in spiritual "I-wonder-land." But if you are seeking to live an impactful SHE life and you know where you're headed, then the direction you go and the decisions you make matter a lot. So how do you know which road to take? By discovering and living out your God-given purpose.

Since the beginning, God made everything on purpose. He created the sky for a reason: to separate the waters of the earth from the waters of the heavens (see Genesis 1:6-8). He made the land with a purpose: so there would be dry ground between the seas for us to live on (Genesis 1:9-10). He designed the sun and moon with a plan in mind: to mark off seasons, days, and years (Genesis 1:14). And as the crowning glory of creation, he made human beings in his own image (Genesis 1:27). So doesn't it make sense that he has a purpose for *you* too?

For everything, absolutely everything, above and below, visible and invisible . . . everything got started in him and finds its purpose in him.
Colossians 1:16, THE MESSAGE

QUIZ: ARE YOU LIVING ON PURPOSE?

Put a check mark next to the statements that describe you.

☐ I'm maintaining—I tend to focus on just getting by.

☐ My life is an endless string of robotically working, sleeping, working, sleeping.

☐ I find myself living for that two weeks of vacation or that perfect guy to sweep me off my feet or that ideal job that will fulfill me and pay me what I'm worth.

☐ Even when I get what I think I want, it never seems to measure up to what I needed or expected.

☐ I try to stay busy to make something of myself—trying to earn, achieve, and qualify.

☐ I equate success with accomplishment.

☐ I measure my achievements by other people's approval and by the recognition I receive. Even when other people think I've got it all together, inside I feel empty and confused.

☐ I have a pretty good idea of why I exist.

☐ I feel called to something bigger than myself, something that keeps coming up in everything I do.

☐ I'm still working to accomplish that thing that gnaws at me down inside, whether or not others commend me for it.

☐ I try to make decisions that help me move toward my goal.

If you have the most check marks in the first list, you find yourself just existing in a **survival mode**. (Note to self: The good life doesn't come through survival mode.)

If you have the most check marks in the middle list, you're stuck in a **success mode**. (Note to self: In the search for purpose, success mode isn't going to cut it.)

If you have the most check marks in the last list, you're well on your way to being in a **significance mode**. (*DingDingDing!* Significance mode is the only way to discover how to really live.)

The LORD has made everything for his own purposes.
Proverbs 16:4

SHE ASKS

CLAIRE (15)

I've made so many mistakes, how can God possibly use me?

REBECCA SAYS

Satan would love to rip you off by trying to make you believe that you are unusable because of your mistakes. Don't let him! If you've confessed your sins to God and asked for his forgiveness, you are free from the weight of your past. A quote that I've often said in my concerts is simply: "God doesn't call the qualified; he qualifies the called." In other words, God can use a willing person, no matter what's in her past. Often he can use our weaknesses as strengths because we rely on him more when we feel weak. We also are more able to relate with other people who are struggling with the same things we have dealt with.

WHAT ON EARTH **ARE YOU HERE FOR?**

Check out what gives Christians their meaning in life. (This list comes from *The Purpose-Driven Life.*)[5]

1. YOU WERE PLANNED FOR GOD'S PLEASURE.
2. YOU WERE FORMED FOR GOD'S FAMILY.
3. YOU WERE CREATED TO BECOME LIKE CHRIST.
4. YOU WERE SHAPED FOR SERVING GOD.
5. YOU WERE MADE FOR A MISSION.

You're here to be part of not only what God is doing in the whole world but also what he wants to do individually through you. He wants you to find and fulfill your purpose.

HOW DO I SIGN UP FOR LIFE-ON-PURPOSE?

Here's the thing. Without Christ, life is pretty shallow and meaningless. The only way to live an on-purpose life is to do life with God. The good news is, he tells us how.

- KNOW HIM.

  You will grow as you learn to know God better and better.

  Colossians 1:10

- LOVE HIM.

  You must love the LORD your God with all your heart, all your soul, and all your strength.

  Deuteronomy 6:5

- FOLLOW HIM.

  [Christ] is your example, and you must follow in his steps.

  1 Peter 2:21

In a wealthy home some utensils are made of gold and silver, and some are made of wood and clay. The expensive utensils are used for special occasions, and the cheap ones are for everyday use. If you keep yourself pure, you will be a special utensil for honorable use. Your life will be clean, and you will be ready for the Master to use you for every good work.

2 Timothy 2:20-21

SHE GETS PERSONAL

What regrets do you have from your past?

....

....

....

What choices have you made that you think messed up God's plans for your life?

....

....

Do you believe he can recreate you, mistakes and all, and use you for his good purpose? What does Romans 8:28 say about this?

....

....

Think of a time you felt God's love, mercy, and forgiveness.

....

....

What aspects of your lifestyle stand between you and God and the fulfillment of his plan for you? Attitudes? Emotions? Motives? Write these down and ask God to forgive and recreate you. Then put them behind you. TODAY IS A NEW DAY.

....

....

GIRL TALK!

Make a bonfire (or cozy up by the fireplace) with a group of your friends. Talk about these questions and others you may come up with. Oh, and don't forget the s'mores.

If you knew tomorrow would be your last day on earth, how would you spend it?

Is there a person or cause you'd be willing to die for?

What legacy would you like to pass on to your kids and grandkids someday?

What do you want people to remember you for?

What's one of your "impossible" dreams for your life—something that can't happen unless God is involved?

FINDING YOUR PURPOSE 101: **PASSION**

Work enthusiastically for the Lord, for you know that nothing you do for the Lord is ever useless.
1 Corinthians 15:58

- What do you enjoy doing the most?
- What breaks your heart?
- What would you like to do if time and money were no object?
- What do you dream about?
- Who do you feel the most compassion for?
- When do you feel the most fulfilled?

FINDING YOUR PURPOSE 201: **GIFTS AND TALENTS**

A man's gift makes room for him and brings him before great men.
Proverbs 18:16, NASB
God has given us different gifts for doing certain things well.
Romans 12:6

- What has God gifted you to do that is different from others you know?
- What do you do well?
- What comes naturally to you at school? at home? with your friends?
- When it comes to your spiritual life, what roles seem to fit with who you were made to be?
- What personality strengths and weaknesses do you observe in yourself? How do they affect your gifts?

SPIRITUAL BIRTHDAY PRESENTS

Do any of these sound like you? (FYI, these are just *some* of the spiritual gifts, so don't sweat it if none of them sound like you.) Check out Romans 12:6-8, I Corinthians 12:7-11, and Ephesians 4:11-13 for more info.

service	I like to work behind the scenes to help people out.
teaching	It comes naturally for me to explain the Bible so that other people get it.
encouragement	I like to build other Christians up and motivate them to go deeper in their faith.
giving	I feel fulfilled when I share what I have (money, energy, stuff).
leadership	People seem to follow me and look to me for guidance.
kindness	I can empathize with people when they are going through rough spots.
wise advice	I'm able to see situations clearly and give people practical, godly advice when they're making decisions.
faith	I can trust God's promises and his presence, even when tough circumstances come my way.
discernment	It's funny, but I seem to be able to tell when an idea is from God and when it's not.
evangelism	I love to share about Christ with people who don't know him.

SHE ASKS
MEREDITH (18)

I always thought I wanted to be a veterinarian. Now as I get closer to college, I'm starting to feel uneasy. I've been taught that when I'm following God's will, I will "feel peace about it." But every time I start to pursue this field, I get an uneasy feeling, and I start thinking about my interest and abilities in photography instead. What should I do?

REBECCA SAYS

When I was a young girl, I had two dreams. One was to work at an orphanage and help children in need, and the other was to be in a musical like *The Sound of Music*. Singing professionally wasn't the biggest dream of my life, but when God started to lead me in that direction, I followed—trusting that he knew what was best for me. In the last few years I've had the chance to fulfill both dreams: by working at an orphanage in Romania, being involved with the ministry of Compassion International, and playing the role of Maggie in the rock opera *!Hero*. God has really shown me that when we are faithful to his leading in our lives, he will fulfill the desires that he has birthed in our hearts for his glory (see Psalm 37:4). God reveals his will to us in a number of ways—first by giving us his peace, then through other avenues such as Christian friends and family, circumstances, and the Bible to speak to our heart.

"You are a vital part of something much bigger than yourself. . . .
Do you sense that your life is a part of God's eternal purposes?"[6]
Henry Blackaby

Taking great photographs · Playing the guitar · Making new people feel comfortable · Running fast · Caring for little kids · Knowing when someone needs to talk · Adding numbers in my head · Je parle français · Patiently explaining things · Keeping my stuff organized · Building a wet-wood fire · Swimming · Writing encouraging notes · Acting and drama · Sewing my own clothes · Fixing computers · Writing funny stories · Driving carefully · Juggling · Memorizing Bible verses · Remembering my friends' birthdays · Building birdhouses · Training puppies · Playing chess · Balancing my checkbook · Decorating cakes · Cleaning a fish tank · Recognizing the good in others · Surfing · Dancing · Making chocolate-chip cookies · Drawing cartoon figures · Speaking in front of crowds · Cheering my friends up · Making good assists

(hockey, soccer, basketball) · Growing flowers (I have a green thumb) · Keeping a great sense of rhythm · Recognizing grammatical errors · Doing prom hairstyles · Performing CPR · Spelling (and defining) *anticoagulant, ocher, bucolic,* and *symposium* · Sailing a sailboat · Trying new foods · Finding the bright side in any situation · Bowling a strike · Painting · Doing all my homework on time · Finding my way in the woods · Making my tongue into a three-leaf clover · Walking on my hands · Singing the entire range of the piano (well . . . I can sing) · Making people laugh · Calligraphy · Crocheting · Decorating my room · Changing the oil in a car · Predicting the stock market · Composing poetry · Convincing people of things · Drawing 3-D pictures · Impersonating others · Brainstorming creative projects · Performing random

THINGS I MIGHT BE GOOD AT

acts of kindness · Finding great bargains · Keeping my promises · Helping out around the house · Finding the perfect gift for someone · Making the perfect gift for someone · Being honest about my feelings · Climbing trees · Designing computer graphics · Improvising on the saxophone · Identifying different bird species · Assembling model planes · Getting out tough stains · Seeing both sides to every story · Following instructions to set up new gadgets · Arranging flowers · Keeping in touch with faraway friends · Maintaining a healthy diet · Riding and showing my horse · Being a good sport (whether I win or lose) · Solving Mensa mind puzzles · Working as a team player · Coming up with long lists of talents people might have · Hanging wallpaper · Wiggling my ears · Thinking creatively · Making cute

scrapbook pages · Communicating effectively with others · Comforting friends who are hurting · Building a strong bridge out of Popsicle sticks · Shooting with a bow and arrow · Guessing how many gumballs are in the jar · Thinking Of Great Acronyms (TOGA) · Saying "NO" to drugs · Preventing forest fires · Being fair to everyone · Making correct change · Peeling apples · Riding a unicycle · Rock climbing · Sympathizing with hurting friends · Serving with a smile · Receiving a compliment · Leading others · Supporting family members · Showing my school spirit · Typing fast · Relaxing · Remembering faces and names · Describing a scene or event to other people · Storytelling · Praising God in creative ways · Organizing · Writing poetry and music · Doing favors for friends and family · Making good iced tea

SHE SPEAKS

LATISHA (17)

A lot of times, people can feel like there's no hope after they've been through something. God can turn that around. Just sharing my story helps make me more understanding of other people and their struggles. I can relate to people better. Part of my purpose is to help people. Just to help redeem people from the mistakes they've made. There is a purpose in everyone's life.

THEY'VE BEEN THERE

Ask your family about what they see as your passions, gifts, and you-forming experiences. What have they observed about you? What do they see that gets you excited? What do they see you doing with your life? (Hey, while you're at it, why not talk to them about their gifts too?)

The LORD has told you what is good, and this is what he requires of you: to do what is right, to love mercy, and to walk humbly with your God.
Micah 6:8

FINDING YOUR PURPOSE 301: **EXPERIENCE**

We know that God causes everything to work together for the good of those who love God and are called according to his purpose for them.
Romans 8:28

- Brainstorm 10 of the most significant events—both good and bad—that have happened in your life. Draw a time line that shows when these things occurred.

_____

- Looking back on these events, can you see a pattern or plan for any of them?

....

....

- What tough stuff have you been through that could help you minister to others during their hardships?

....

....

....

FINDING YOUR PURPOSE 401: **PLAN**

How can I use my passions, my gifts and talents, and my experiences now?

- With friends
- At school
- At home
- At church
- At work
- Other:_____

How can I use my passions, my gifts and talents, and my experiences in the future?

- In choosing a career
- In making life decisions
- At church
- At work
- In relationships

Don't copy the behavior and customs of this world, but let God transform you into a new person by changing the way you think. Then you will learn to know God's will for you, which is good and pleasing and perfect.
Romans 12:2

SHE SPEAKS

ADRIENNE (16)

Purpose will come if I'm following God and walking with him. It's a choice. It's my choice whether or not I walk with God. I need to be in his Word daily. I need to live the life he wants me to. If I don't choose the right way, I'm stuck with the consequences. If I don't, that's what I've chosen for myself.

YOUR LIFE **MISSION STATEMENT**

A. WHO ARE YOU?

B. WHY ARE YOU?

C. WHAT DO YOU STAND FOR?

STEP 1: *ID your successes.* Identify four examples where you have had personal success recently. These successes could be at school, at church, in your community, at home, etc. Write them down.

1. ....

2. ....

3. ....

4. ....

Is there a common theme—or themes—to these examples?

STEP 2: *ID your values.* On a separate page, come up with a list of attributes that identify who you are and what your priorities are. The list can be as long as you need. Now see if you can narrow the list down to the five or six most important values. Is there one value that is the most important to you?

....

....

....

STEP 3: *ID your contributions.* How can you make a difference? In an ideal situation, how could you contribute best to:

• the world in general?
• your friends?
• your family?
• your school?
• your future employers/employees?
• your community?
• your church?

STEP 4: *ID your goals.* Make a list of your personal goals: short-term (up to three years) and long-term (beyond three years).

Short-term goals: ....

....

....

Long-term goals: ....

....

....

STEP 5: Based on the first four steps and a better understanding of yourself, write a draft of your personal mission statement.

....

....

THE BUZZ ON A BIBLE SHE

QUEEN ESTHER

LITTLE ORPHAN ESTHER TO MISS PERSIA:

Esther was a Jewish orphan who had been raised by her cousin Mordecai. She lived a pretty ordinary life (for the 400s BC, anyway) until (drum roll, please . . .) the Miss Persia Pageant. The king had a contest that would rival any reality TV show, and the winner would walk away with the royal crown. After a year of beauty treatments, designer clothes, and a special diet, Esther was declared the winner! She suddenly found herself transported from Jewish orphan to queen of Persia.

But it was no happily-ever-after for the newlyweds. The king's most powerful official, Haman, hated Jews. When Mordecai refused to bow before anyone except God, Haman blew his top. He built a gallows to hang Mordecai on, and he plotted to destroy all the other Jews in the Persian empire.

BRAINS AND BEAUTY:

Esther had kept her Jewish heritage a secret from her husband and the people of the kingdom, but now it was time for her to intervene.

UNDER PENALTY OF DEATH:

And intervention meant Esther would have to reveal her Jewish heritage to the king. How would he react? Would he feel she had deceived him? Did he hate the Jews as much as Haman did? Then there was that other little problem—no one was allowed to go before the king without being summoned, not even the queen. If the king didn't spare her, she'd be killed.

But Mordecai urged her on. "Who knows whether you have come to the kingdom for such a time as this?" he said. Esther realized that if she remained silent, she might miss God's plan for her—and her people. After days of prayer, Esther dressed like a million bucks and walked into the presence of the king. She took a deep breath, knowing it could be her last.

THE FATE OF A NATION:

A hush fell over the room. Then slowly, ever so slowly, the king raised his golden scepter as proof that her life was safe. He asked, "What is your request, Queen Esther? It will be granted to you."

The first part of her prayer had been answered. Her life had been spared. But just as she recognized that God had a plan for her, she also recognized that he would accomplish it in his own time. When Esther felt it was time to make her request, she pleaded with the king for the lives of her people. Her timing was right. Her persuasion was effective. And her God was big enough to save a nation.

FOR SUCH A TIME AS THIS:

The course of history had been changed. Instead of killing the Jews, many people converted to the faith of the Jews when they saw the providence of their God. And God used Esther to save his chosen people. He knew he could count on her to fulfill her purpose, so his bigger purpose would also be fulfilled.

WANT MORE DETAILS?

For the whole scoop, check out Esther 1–10.

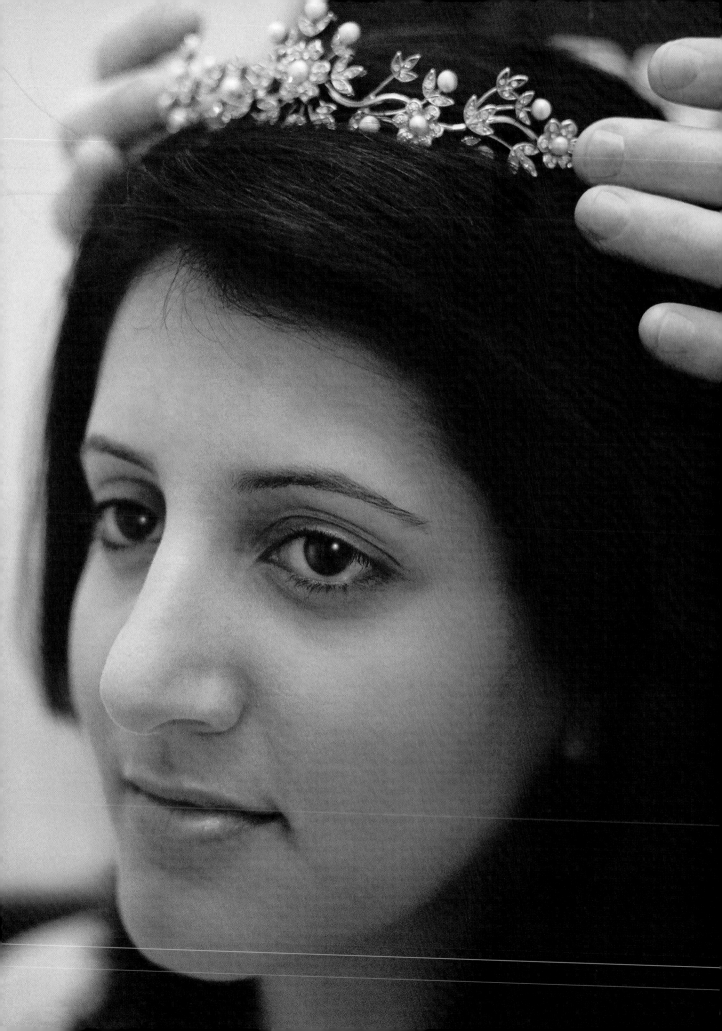

REBECCA SAYS

When I was 14, my family and I moved from Australia to the United States. My dad had accepted a job in Nashville, Tennessee, so my parents, my five brothers, and I began our American adventure. At the time, my parents thought they knew what God's purpose was in bringing us to a new country and a new life, but after a few months, we were unsure. My dad's promised job fell through, and we were left with no income, no furniture, no car, eight mouths to feed, and another baby on the way. During the coming months, we had to rely on God like never before. We prayed for our needs and saw checks arrive in the mail unexpectedly. Doors opened for us to make money by cleaning houses, raking yards, and babysitting. Food and furniture appeared on our doorstep. One family gave us a minivan the same day they met us.

Through the struggle and triumph of those times, God gave a 15-year-old girl a message to share that prayer is powerful and that God still does miracles when you trust him. Now, over a decade later, that grown-up girl travels around the world sharing about God's hope through music. My dad has a thriving Christian management company, and my three eldest brothers are serving God in their respective ministries.

Our family came to America knowing that God had called us here, but God had a greater purpose for us than we could have dreamed.

HERE ARE SOME EXAMPLES OF PERSONAL MISSION STATEMENTS FROM REAL-LIFE SHEs:

"To serve God through showing compassion to others, and to give God the glory in whatever I am doing."

MEGHAN (19)

"When you looked at me, did you see Jesus?"

ELLIE (29)

"To wisely live a life of love, making the most of every opportunity" (based on Ephesians 5:15-16).

LINNEA (25)

"To use my gifts and experiences to expand the Kingdom of Christ."

DIANA (21)

"To act justly, love mercy, and walk humbly with my God" (based on Micah 6:8).

BAILEY (27)

"To bring Christ's joy to others."

ANNA (20)

"To make a positive difference in the world by loving God above everything else and allowing his love to flow through me."

EMILE (21)

"I want to be someone who does not settle for a mediocre Christian life—I desire to live a radical life with Jesus. This means loving God and others well. This also means seeking to live out my life verse: 'I don't care about my own life. The most important thing is that I complete my mission, the work that the Lord Jesus gave me—to tell people the Good News about God's grace' (Acts 20:24, NCV)."

REBECCA ST. JAMES

SHEism: The truly purposeful SHE understands her unique calling and uses her abilities and gifts effectively for the glory of God.

WHAT'S YOUR SHE SIGN?

You see it all the time in magazines. It's your horoscope, and it supposedly tells your fortune according to when you were born. As Christians, we can throw those lying horoscopes away and concentrate on the *real* signs.

Now that you're God's SHE girl, you'll want others to recognize the signs of the new—and improved—you. How will they know?

Begin today in whatever month you're in. Over the next year, pay attention to each of these SHE signs we talked about throughout the book. Ask God to bring this particular sign alive for you during the month. In the space below each month, write down the ways God is working in your life in each of these areas.

SECURE JANUARY	**CONNECTED** FEBRUARY	**FEMININE** MARCH

Those who fear the LORD are secure. Proverbs 14:26	A friend is always loyal. Proverbs 17:17	A gentle and quiet spirit . . . is so precious to God. 1 Peter 3:4
What God is doing	What God is doing	What God is doing

SAFE
APRIL

[The Lord] alone is
my refuge, my place
of safety.
Psalm 91:2

What God is doing

BEAUTIFUL
MAY

People judge by
outward appearance,
but the LORD looks
at the heart.
1 Samuel 16:7

What God is doing

PURE
JUNE

Keep yourself pure.
1 Timothy 5:22

What God is doing

FREE
JULY

You will know the truth,
and the truth
will set you free.
John 8:32

What God is doing

HEALTHY
AUGUST

Refuse to worry,
and keep your body healthy.
Ecclesiastes 11:10

What God is doing

GUIDED
SEPTEMBER

Older women
must train the younger women . . .
to live wisely and be pure.
Titus 2:4-5

What God is doing

BOUNDARIED
OCTOBER

The boundary lines
have fallen for me
in pleasant places.
Psalm 16:6, NIV

What God is doing

....
....
....
....
....
....
....
....
....

PURPOSEFUL
NOVEMBER

"I know the plans I have for you,"
says the LORD. "They are plans
for good and not for disaster,
to give you a future and a hope."

Jeremiah 29:11

What God is doing

EMPOWERED
DECEMBER

God's power is working in us.
2 Corinthians 6:7

What God is doing

....
....
....
....
....
....
....
....
....

ENDNOTES

WHO IS SHE?

1. The Barna Group, "The Barna Update: The Year's Most Intriguing Findings" (December 12, 2000), http://www.barna.org/FlexPage.aspx?Page=BarnaUpdate&BarnaUpdateID=77.

2. A. P. MacKay, L. A. Fingerhut, and C. R. Duran, *Adolescent Health Chartbook* (Hyattsville, Md.: National Center for Health Statistics, 2000), http://www.cdc.gov/nchs/data/hus/hus00.pdf.

3. Wanda Franz et al., "Adolescent Abortion," Association for Interdisciplinary Research in Values and Social Change (Fall 1990), http://www.lifeissues.net/writers/air/air_vol3no3_19901.html.

SECURE

1. J. Toth, "New Study of Domestic Violence Finds Mandatory Arrests Backfire," *Los Angeles Times*, 18 December 1991, A5.

2. E. Kessner, "Sweetheart Murders: When Teen Boyfriends Turn into Killers," *Redbook*, March 1988, 130.

3. D. G. Kilpatrick et al., *Rape in America: A Report to the Nation 1992*, National Victim Center (Arlington, Virginia) and the Medical University of South Carolina, Crime Victims Research and Treatment Center (Charleston).

4. Rape, Abuse & Incest National Network, "RAINN Statistics," http://www.rainn.org/statistics.html.

5. Lindsey Tanner, "Violence: Young Girls Victimized by Their Dates," Associated Press, July 31, 2001, http://www.tgorski.com/Violence/Violence%20-%20Young%20Girls%20Victimized%20by%20Their%20Dates%20010801.htm.

6. Harris Interactive Survey (1997), http://www.harrisinteractive.com/.

7. Suzanne Ageton, *Sexual Assault among Adolescents* (Lexington, Mass.: Lexington Books, 1983).

8. David Bamber, "Pedophiles Calling a Fifth of Children on Net," *Telegraph* (March 12, 2000), http://news.telegraph.co.uk/news/main.jhtml?xml=/news/2000/12/03/npaed03.xml.

9. "Recent Statistics on Internet Dangers," from the Pew Study reported in *JAMA* (2001), http://www.protectkids.com/dangers/stats.htm.

10. New Jersey Department of Community Affairs, Division on Women, "Male and Female Rights and Responsibilities in a Dating Relationship" and Nebraska Domestic Violence Sexual Assault Coalition, "Reaching and Teaching Teens to Stop Violence."

CONNECTED

1. Andrew Brown, "Romancing the Phone" (September 15, 2004), http://www.cnn.com/2004/TECH/09/15/sp.phone.romance/.

2. The Barna Group, "Americans Identify What They Want Out of Life" (2000), http://www.barna.org/FlexPage.aspx?Page=BarnaUpdate&BarnaUpdateID=57.

BEAUTIFUL

1. MTV, *I Want a Famous Face*, see http://www.mtv.com/onair/i_want_a_famous_face/.

2. ANRED: Anorexia Nervosa and Related Eating Disorders, Inc., "Statistics: How Many People Have Eating Disorders?" http://www.anred.com/stats.html.

3. "March Is Women's History Month: Application of the Critical Theory," http://www127.pair.com/critical/food-14.htm.

4. Media Awareness Network, "Media and Girls," http://www.media-awareness.ca/english/issues/stereotyping/women_and_girls/women_girls.cfm.

5. National Institute on Media and the Family, "Fact Sheet: Media's Effect on Girls: Body Image and Gender Identity," http://www.mediafamily.org/facts/facts_mediaeffect.shtml.

6. *UCB Devotional* (Australia: United Christian Broadcasters, n.d.), 39. Author and copyright date unknown.

7. CM Central, "Artist Database: Bethany Dillon Biography," http://www.cmcentral.com/artists/882.html.

PURE

1. Doug Herman, *Come Clean* (Wheaton, Ill.: Tyndale House Publishers, 2004), 35.

2. Centers for Disease Control and Prevention, "Tracking the Hidden Epidemics: Trends in STDs in the United States 2000," http://www.cdc.gov/nchstp/dstd/Stats_Trends/Trends2000.pdf.

3. Herman, *Come Clean*, 56.

4. CDC, "Tracking the Hidden Epidemics," 4.

5. Ibid.

FROM THE EDITOR

Remember Mary of Bethany? When Jesus came to visit her home, Mary's sister was busy doing other things. But Mary sat at his feet, soaking in Jesus' every word. Learning what pleased him. Living her life around his principles. And when her sister complained that Mary wasn't helping her with the chores, Jesus said,

"Mary has chosen that good part, which will not be taken away from her" (Luke 10:42, NKJV).

If you could hear Jesus speak today, he might just say similar words to you.

By choosing to read this book and take these nine rules to guide your life seriously, you've chosen the good part. It's not like the rules are ever going to change, and it's for sure that the girls who follow them will always win in the end.

I am so proud of you. More important, Jesus is proud of you. Keep keeping his rules, and keep sitting at his feet. He has much more to teach you and some wonderful places to lead you in your life. After all, you've chosen the good part, and that can never be taken away from you.

Love,

Lynda

6. National Center for Injury Prevention and Control, "WISQARS Leading Causes of Death Reports, 1999–2002," http://webapp.cdc.gov/sasweb/ncipc/leadcaus10.html.

7. Centers for Disease Control and Prevention, "Trends in Sexual Risk Behaviors among High School Students: United States, 1991–2001" (September 27, 2002), http://www.cdc.gov/mmwr/preview/mmwrhtml/mm5138a2.htm.

8. Noelle Howey, "Oral Report," *Seventeen*, August 2003.

9. Child Trends DataBank, "Sexually Experienced Teens," http://www.childtrendsdatabank.org/pdf/24_PDF.pdf.

FREE

1. Online Guide to Offbeat Attractions, "Floyd Collins: America's Greatest Doomed Cave Explorer," http://www.roadsideamerica.com/attract/KYCAVfloyd.html; James M. Deem, "Floyd Collins: Trapped in Sand Cave," http://www.jamesmdeem.com/cavestory2.htm; and Gateway to Mammoth, "History of Cave City," http://www.cavecity.com/history-floyd.asp.

2. Jackelyn Barnard, "Teens Doing Self-Mutilation to Deal with Stress," *First Coast News*, 6 July 2004, http://www.firstcoastnews.com/news/local/news-article.aspx?storyid=21004.

3. Centers for Disease Control and Prevention, National Center for Injury Prevention and Control, "Suicide: Fact Sheet," http://www.cdc.gov/ncipc/factsheets/suifacts.htm.

4. Centers for Disease Control and Prevention, Tobacco Information and Prevention Source, "Teens and Tobacco: Facts Not Fiction," http://www.cdc.gov/tobacco/tips_4_youth/factfict.htm.

5. Centers for Disease Control and Prevention, National Center for Injury Prevention and Control, "Youth Violence: Fact Sheet," http://www.cdc.gov/ncipc/factsheets/yvfacts.htm.

6. Deborah Epstein, "Welcoming Adolescents to Your Practice," *Medical Economics*, Obstetrics and Gynecologists Edition (1999).

GUIDED

1. Howard G. Hendricks and William D. Hendricks, *As Iron Sharpens Iron: Building Character in a Mentoring Relationship* (Chicago: Moody Press, 1995), 63.

BOUNDARIED

1. Denise Witmer, "Teenagers and Sleep," http://parentingteens.about.com/cs/teensandsleep/a/teenssleepwell.htm.

2. Young Americans Center for Financial Education, "Financial Literacy Statistics," http://yacenter.org/index.cfm?fuseAction=financialLiteracyStatistics.financialLiteracyStatistics.

3. Cult Hotline and Clinic, "Cult Questions and Answers," http://www.cultclinic.org/qa2.html.

4. Mark Moring, ed., *Walk* (Wheaton, Ill.: Tyndale House Publishers, 2003), 88.

5. "Jessica Style: Your Guide to Jessica Simpson's Clothes," http://www.jessicastyle.com (accessed November 2004).

PURPOSEFUL

1. Freedom's Nest Quotes, "Quotes on Meaning in Life," http://www.freedomsnest.com/cgi-bin/q.cgi?subject=meaninginlife.

2. "Simpsons Offer 'Moral Orientation,'" *BBC News*, February 3, 2002, http://news.bbc.co.uk/2/hi/uk_news/scotland/1799183.stm.

3. Quotations come from a number of sources. Mary-Kate and Ashley Olsen: Thomas Chau, "Interview: Mary-Kate and Ashley Olsen from *New York Minute*," *Cinema Confidential News*, April 30, 2004, http://www.cinecon.com/news.php?id=0404301. Tupac Shakur: Famous Quotes, http://home.att.net/~quotations/celebrity.html. Arnold Schwarzenegger: Said What, "The Meaning of Life," http://www.saidwhat.co.uk/articles/meaningoflife.php. Mark Ruffalo: Dotson Rader, "I Wouldn't Give Any of It Back," *Parade*, 9 May 2004, http://archive.parade.com/2004/0509/0509_mark_ruffalo.html. Orlando Bloom: Allison Glock, "Orlando's Magic," *GQ*, January 2004, http://www.theorlandobloomfiles.com/articles/gq04jan.html.

4. Richard T. Kinnier et al., "What Eminent People Have Said about the Meaning of Life," *Journal of Humanistic Psychology* 43, no. 1 (Winter 2003).

5. Rick Warren, *The Purpose-Driven Life* (Grand Rapids, Mich.: Zondervan, 2002).

6. Henry Blackaby, *Experiencing God Day by Day: A Devotional and Journal* (Nashville: Broadman & Holman, 1997), 317.

FROM THE PHOTOGRAPHER: **AUSTYN ELIZABETH BRUENNING**

I was born in Charlotte, North Carolina, and I currently live in Chicago where I am studying photography at Harrington College of Design. Since I was young, I've always loved making art, in whatever media possible. It was only three years ago that I took my first photography class in high school. There was something different with photography than the other mediums I loved. I did not have to work at photography; it came very naturally to me, and as I learned more, I fell more in love with it. During my junior year of high school, I received first place for black-and-white photography in the school art show. I then took a college course during my senior year at a local community college while I was working as an assistant for a commercial photographer.

After I was already enrolled at Harrington College in a program that was not photography, it hit me, *What am I doing?* One month before school started, I switched my major to the photography program at Harrington. I am so thankful that I did. I then received the opportunity of taking the photographs for this book. I was fresh out of high school and took on a project that would display around 200 of my photos—I was in awe. There are so many things God has been doing in my life and all around me. One year ago I never would have thought that I would be going to school for photography, and now I will have a published copy of a small part of my work. All I can do is praise God; he has opened so many doors for me that I would not have been able to open on my own.

I can't forget to introduce Ellie May, my dog and trusted companion. She pretty much fills the largest portion of my life right now. She is a one-and-a-half-year-old white lab and golden retriever mix and is as vocal as they come. She will talk to you for hours on end without your consent to do so. She is a great dog and usually comes with me wherever and whenever possible. There are more glimpses of her throughout the book.

Besides my time at school and with Ellie, I work at Lake Geneva Youth Camp in Wisconsin. I work full-time in the summer and on weekends during the school year. I help run a variety of outdoor activities, including lifeguarding, and I work with the kitchen staff as a waitress/hostess in our dining rooms. My favorite part of the day up at camp—well, anywhere—is seeing the sunset and the stars appear. That's the time I am most awestruck by God and where I will stand for moments and praise him for his creation. Every time I'm able to catch the sun setting it reminds me of how much I really am in his hands. There is no way in the world I would be where I am if there were no God. Even though I forget many times and doubt his strength and unconditional love, the sun will set on that day, and I will be struck with awe and wonder at his glorious works. Never let go, even in those dark times when God seems so faint. He is still holding your hand and leading you through the valley we call life. Never forget that.

nonfiction.

WonkaMania 1-4143-0546-X

The Way I See It 0-8423-0491-6

SHE Teen 1-4143-0028-X

from
Sarah Arthur:

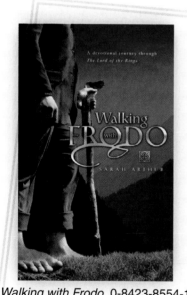

Walking with Frodo 0-8423-8554-1

Walking with Bilbo 1-4143-0131-6

Dating Mr. Darcy 1-4143-0132-4

tap into life.

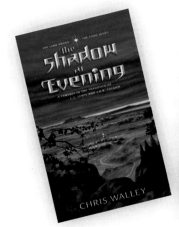

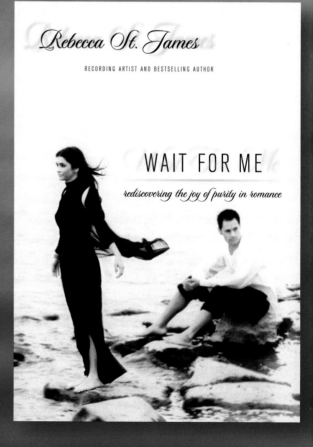

Smart girls still believe in love.

Best-selling author Sarah Arthur shares timeless tips on dating and romance from Jane Austen's classic romantic comedy *Pride and Prejudice.*

Dating Mr. Darcy: The Smart Girl's Guide to Sensible Romance

AVAILABLE NOW AT A BOOKSTORE NEAR YOU!

ISBN 1-4143-0132-4
$9.99

Ever wish you knew the rules for love?

Jake, Mattie, and Emma have been friends forever.
Now Jake and Mattie are going off to college, and
Emma is staying behind. Emma makes them promise
they will share with her what they learn about love.
Every week. The Love Rules.

*Find out what these three learn about love,
relationships, and each other.*

Love Rules
Available now at a bookstore near you!
ISBN 0-8423-8727-7
$9.99